Contents

Dedication

To the heart of our team, the woman of my dreams, Liliana, who along with being the wife for whom I waited so long, is the mother of our greatest treasures, Brian, Kevin, Jason and Megan.

And to all our beloved young people who do not allow the system to dictate what they must say or do.

Acknowledgements

My most sincere thanks to all of those dear pastors who have supported me as well as those who did not – they matured me.

To Claudio Freidzon, my beloved pastor, thanks for the incredible relationship that we have maintained for so many years. I never forget those who bless me.

To Italo Frigoli, you are a classic in my books. May God continue to give you wonderful messages.

To José Vera; what a pleasure to know you and to enjoy your incredible assistance and unconditional camaraderie in my life.

To Enrique Montenegro, my great friend, thanks for seeing value in me and for investing so many hours of your time.

To our eternal God, thanks for hiring me in the 11th hour and for allowing me to play in the big leagues; I can never repay my debt to you.

Introduction

The boxer climbs into the ring aware that this could be his last fight. There is much more at stake than just a prize belt, a mere symbol of the dedication that forges a heavyweight champion. He is risking his reputation, his life, and his future. He knows he must rise to the occasion, to hit and then hit again. He must not spare any effort when the time comes to strike. We are not, in case you were not aware, talking about another movie staging of the Rocky Balboa saga. No, this is real life. A "knockout" at this point in his career could do much more than leave him stretched out on the canvas. It could push him down into the ranks of anonymity, to a bitter headline in the tabloids, to bland mediocrity. With twenty seconds to go before the bell, the boxer has reached a point of no return. He must not lose. He cannot afford that luxury. Winning is everything for him, it is the only thing.

The goalie takes a deep breath. The crowd is screaming uncontrollably — both cheers and jeers. The player stands silently in front of the waiting goalkeeper. He has twenty seconds to kick the ball. At some other time or place he could miss the goal and the result would be just another forgettable moment for football fans. But now he is not playing with that option. This is the first playoff game in a world championship. At stake is the golden International Cup; and in the big leagues there is no margin for error. His team has "gold" fever and is counting on his effectiveness, his precision. The one hundred thousand spectators seem to be moving in slow motion. He is not playing just a simple game – what is important is not merely another competition. At stake is a million-dollar European contract, his password to a secure future. He is an integral part of the team and of the outcome of the match for all of the people around the world who are watching via satellite. The pressure is on. He thirsts for victory.

If he falls, the boxer will get up from the mat, but his prestige and reputation will not. If the soccer player misses the goal, he may lament on the field but someone else will be tearing up the unsigned contract.

In Buenos Aires, at Boca Juniors Stadium, 70,000 people are crammed into the stands of the huge football stadium. The grassy field is covered with crowds of young people who have come from all over the country. There are only two minutes left before nine o'clock at night, the starting time of a massive crusade event, the "Super Classic for Young People," following a lengthy tour of the entire nation. The noise is deafening, the atmosphere electrifying. For some curious reason, everything here looks like it is moving in slow motion.

Just two days earlier, this very same stadium was the site of a rock concert that brought together some of the best artists of the genre. Promoters expected the stadium would be filled, but only 15,000 fans attended. Today, only two days later, in the same place and using exactly the same equipment, 70,000 teens have gathered to worship Jesus. Journalists are there to make sneering comparisons but they are as surprised and excited as everyone else at the turnout.

One of them, a reporter from one of the most important television news programs in the country, intercepts me I am about to go on stage. The question is predictable, almost obvious. Images from the rock concert held two days ago still reverberate in local minds.

"How do you feel, knowing that Christian young people have filled this stadium beyond its capacity, outperforming one of the most well promoted rock concerts ever held in the nation?"

While the journalist speaks, some images from the evangelistic tour are showing on enormous, gigantic screens next to the stage and the crowd is screaming wildly. It is almost impossible to converse with the journalist, but he insists.

"Has faith defeated rock music?"

I liked the word "defeated." I do not have anything against rock music, and I almost could not hear what the reporter was saying, but I was fascinated with the idea of winning a battle. The crowd applauds, making human "waves," awaiting a great victory.

"I am a poor loser," I replied.

"What?" he asked, putting the microphone in front of my mouth.

"I said that I do not like to lose. We have decided that we will win this championship of life. These people want to beat the system," I said, waving toward the stadium, "and in fact they are going to make it. For us, we always win."

The stadium lights dim and flashing spotlights highlight people who are raising their hands and clapping. A countdown appears on the screen — there are only seconds left before the program is to begin.

"Just one more question," he says. "Tell me what you are feeling right now, just before you go out on the platform."

My wife takes my hand, a dozen technicians are running around nervously, and someone is giving a signal to the cameras that will broadcast this crusade event live to twenty-two countries of Latin America.

I am seconds away from going onstage to preach to 70,000 young people who thirst eagerly for victory, for passion. But even so I want to answer this inquisitive journalist, perhaps because I am feeling the same pressure and responsibility that any fighter might be feeling, the same adrenalin rush of any competitive player who strives to surpass his own record. I am not playing a game, but I still do not like to lose. I thirst for spiritual "gold" — I possess a double dose of spiritual ambition. I feel like I am walking five centimeters above the ground — because I do not want to be a poor loser. These are the big leagues. Mediocrity holds no appeal for me, I am not content to be just another face in the crowd — I am going for the championship.

No one remembers the person who finished eighth or even second place. Those who say that the only thing what matters is having a chance to compete were probably never winners drunk with winning. I want the best that God has for me. I am aiming for the gold medal. I am not interested in winning the amateur contest; I do not want to play on the beginners' team. I do not want to be satisfied with the silver medal or excuse myself by thinking the bronze medal is not so bad. I do not want to settle for at least not coming in last. I want victory. A crushing victory. I want to be the worst nightmare that hell ever had.

A speaker interrupts my thoughts. He is announcing the beginning of the Superclassic Youth Convention at Boca Juniors Stadium. The music is vibrant, explosive. Thousands of young adults and teenagers begin to sing. But the persistent journalist is still waiting for an answer. If I tell him that I want to win, he will think that this is all about personal glory. He is waiting for my response before headlining his report. To him, I am an "electronic televangelist," a "multimedia messiah," or maybe even a skilled manipulator of the masses. He does not understand anything about spiritual warfare or about motivating an entire counterculture to become people of integrity. He does not know anything about victories, does not understand what it feels like to be a champion. He cannot imagine what it is like to muster one last punch while struggling for breath in the final moments of the fight. He has never been under pressure to either win or die. I ask myself how I can explain to him what it means to serve God. The answer is too complicated for a single sentence. There are so many code phrases that this journalist would never understand.

"I feel like I am writing history," I reply.

Finally, the journalist steps aside and allows me to continue toward the stage. He is satisfied.

The historic Boca Juniors stadium shines brightly on this hot night in Buenos Aires. Thousands of voices intone a song that says: "When this church worships you, your power is released from heaven." Fireworks explode before the uplifted faces of thousands of young people who have traveled many long hours to be here tonight. We are winning another battle. We feel elated, as if clinching another goal in the decisive final moments of a World Cup game and coming from behind to a surprise victory over a rival.

The first minute of the rest of my life has just begun.

CHAPTER 1

HEART OF A NOBLEMAN

"Boy, God will never use a person like you."

The man was furious, evincing no pity as he pointed at me with his bony finger. The words were harsh as a stone, cutting, categorical. His German accent was heavier than usual, perhaps because his anxiety was deeply rooted. The pastor was angry and his condemnation would handicap my life for a long time. A phrase like that makes a 15-year-old boy feel like failure defines him.

In essence, this is a book of secret codes — of those things that you had always wanted to ask but never dared.

Perhaps you came to believe that you are the only one with this hidden syndrome.

Do you want to know what happens in the heart of a young person with this type of complex? Follow the example of myself, your servant, and observe me at the tender age of fifteen. What that German patriarch said had some truth to it — I was not behaving as a member of God's great team.

From the age of twelve I had a problem getting enough to eat, along with the inevitable growth spurt that happens during a boy's adolescence. I was taking a variety of vitamin pills, but nothing helped me gain even one miserable pound of weight. My skinny legs literally looked like those of an ostrich, my knees like knobs sticking out of my short pants. A rather prominent nose and protruding eyes were also among the physical characteristics that, together, made me a very introverted person whose inner world was in chaos. Do not discount what I am trying to say. Only those who have walked this path in their own lives can fully understand and look back with a wry smile.

Those horrifying gaffes that made you a "nerd" (know-it-all) — unpopular and detested by your peers. The belly bulging over your belt, even though you tried to hide it by standing up straight and raising your chin. Those crooked yellow teeth (I know this is unpleasant but it helps to remember). The special shoes for flat feet. The enormous ears that you could not flatten or hide under your hair. Those frustrating tremors in the throat, the sudden loss of voice whenever you tried to speak in public. The sudden squeaks in the voice of a teenager and the pimples, oh, those terrorizing intruders that threatened to ruin your face and the rest of your reputation. Have you been there? If you recognize that bitter place of disorientation and damaged self-esteem, I am sure that your smile may be tinged with a certain aura of pain and nostalgia.

I still remember my nickname in high school. It really bothered me. Every time they called me by that name, I would get angry. My body was so thin, so fragile in appearance, that they dubbed me "Dead Man."

When it came time to choose teams for a sports competition, no one wanted the "Dead Man" in their ranks.

"He doesn't even know how to run," they would say.

"It's not that he doesn't know how, he just can't … he's already dead, he's pale, his complexion is colorless."

When it came time for jokes, one fat boy whose own self-esteem was torn to shreds and myself, the "Dead Man," were the perfect targets for rotten jokes.

But the worst came during the summer – three long and feverish months of torture. I would try to find ingenious ways to avoid wearing short pants. These only accentuated even more my thin and rickety-looking legs. To someone with an adolescent complex, extremely hot weather matters little. Long sleeves provided a refuge for skeletal arms. Overdressing always seems like a shield from acid jokes and piercing looks.

If you add to that the pathetic words of a pastor who, filled with rage, points you out with his index finger and reminds you that you don't fit on God's team, then you no longer live, you only try to survive.

If at fifteen years of age your whole world is of the opinion that you are "dead," the future does not seem very encouraging.

Fortunately, history tells us that many "dead" people decided to change their destiny.

YOUR NOBLE SHIELD

—Someday, I would like to be one of the king's knights, —a little blond boy says as he watches a military parade.

—Ha, ha, ha! A knight? The son of a roofer wants to be a knight! — An elderly and quarrelsome neighbor mocks the dreams of the ambitious little boy. —It would be easier to change the stars than to make you a knight.

The child feels a sting from this dart of common sense. Logic says that he is not of noble birth. The neighbor has already said what everyone knows: he is the son of a roofer, just a man who repairs leaks.

Nevertheless, the young boy has a hope, tenuous though it is, but still he has hope. He is the boxer who has lost every round and yet is prepared to fight one more round. He is the runner who sprains his ankle fifty feet away from the finish line but continues to run.

—Will I be able to change the stars someday? —he asks his father.

—If you really want to, you can change your star —the wise roofer replies.

The movie titled "A Knight's Tale" tells the story of some-one who was able to change his destiny. He defied logic and common sense. He should have been a roofer, but he pre-ferred to become a knight. He participated in combat as if he were of noble lineage and won many victories so that by the time they learn that he does not have royal blood, he is already too popular and a recognized champion. Finally, a king hands him the title he has truly earned. The heart of a lion can change your future even when you are "dead."

You can change your destiny.

"You can make it difficult for me to become a doctor," Patch Adams told the commission composed of distinguished doctors. "You can fire me from the medical school faculty. You can rescind my diploma. But I will still be a doctor in my heart. You cannot break my will. You cannot stop a hurricane. I will always be there. You must decide whether you want to have a colleague … or a thorn in your side."

The doctors listened to the aspiring doctor in stunned silence. This man had been able, in only a few months, using the unorthodox method of humor, tending to the patients' emotional well-being as well as physical ailments, to cure many people. Again we see the same common denominator: You are not worthy. You are only a roofer. But people who are determined to change their destiny cannot be broken, and Patch Adams went on to become one of the most well-known specialists in the world. He founded his own medical facility, and his influence later spread around the planet with the discovery of revolutionary new therapy methods that he shared with the medical world.

Do you want to hear another fascinating story? What do you think about being able to sit down in a comfortable theater seat to enjoy watching a full-length movie that the most well-known screenwriters in Hollywood failed to capture? Relax and observe.

A man waits in the silence of a prison cell. An annoying drop of water falls on the harsh concrete. The heat is oppressive and humid, but in these extreme circumstances, the temperature is the least of his worries. Flies are mercilessly swarming all around him, but he doesn't have the energy to swat them away. In any event, they may be the only companion-ship worthy of mention. The other men regard him with sus-picion. They watch him warily. To be honest, the last few months have been very difficult for this quiet prisoner. His brothers hated him with all their hearts and set a trap for him — a classic family quarrel that ended in tragedy, in deeply rooted resentments.

The man is barely a shadow of the boy who once sported an impeccably tailored suit of Italian designer brand, and exuded a delicate aroma of French perfume. Now he is dressed in rags, a sort of loincloth. It is said in the cellblock that he is marked for disgrace. He could have been free — he had risen to become the supervisor for an important magnate. But the gossips say that he made a pass at the beautiful wife of the millionaire. At the time he denied the charge. He has denied the accusation, but "he cannot expect us to believe that it was she who sexually assaulted him," they opined.

"And if it was as he says, he should have slept with her," says the old recluse they called 'The Greek.' "One night of pleasure might have given him his passport to freedom."

The mysterious man continues to recline against the dirty walls of the prison cell. It is almost as if he knows something the others do not. He behaves as though he were represent-ed by a clever attorney who will appeal his sentence, or else perhaps he senses that death is near and will bring relief from so much unjust suffering. He smiles in the silence, dis-playing no agitation. Technically he is dead, without hope. But he no longer feels the heat nor does he seem annoyed with his shackles. It is almost as if he can see through the moldy walls of the cell. The other prisoners assume that he is on the brink of insanity. But the man waits expectantly, as one who believes that he can still change his star. He takes the prison cell as part of the plan, as the final step towards the future.

The squeaky metal doors of the cellblock are pushed open and two guards enter the room. They are searching for the man. One of the guards says in a deep, guttural voice: "Pharaoh wants to see you. He has had a dream and he has heard that you can interpret dreams."

The prisoner does not seem surprised. He climbs the steps that will take him forever from the prison cell, but he is silent.

The other prisoners watch the man's back as he walks away and disappears. If they have the good fortune to live, the next time they see him he will be appareled in the royal robes of a king, resembling a Pharaoh. The magnate will rue the day that he dismissed the man. The wife will confess that she accused him out of spite, unjustly. And his family will bow before him to beg for mercy. The prisoners will regard him as a legend.

His old cellmate, 'The Greek,' will boast and lie: "I knew him when he was a master of nothing but we always knew he would go far. I always knew."

Joseph will rule the nation, occupying a presidential throne and administering the granaries of Egypt. He would learn to win, to experience the thrill of victory.

You, too, can change your star.

You only need to live from the inside out, with an unbroken spirit. Be lion-hearted. Take by surprise those photographers who specialize only on the most famous faces. The commentators and ethical commissioners will not be able to explain where you came from — you have no record, you were dead. Perhaps they were expecting a cypress tree to burn, but there is only a burning bush. Logic says that you should have died a fisherman in the remote village of Capernaum, but your passing shadow heals the sick. They have placed cameras and mobile television equipment around the palace preparing for a satellite broadcast around the world, but the king decides to be born in a stable.

"You can deny me a diploma from the Biblical seminary. You can keep me from obtaining a ministerial license, but I will still be a preacher in my heart. You cannot break my will. You cannot stop a hurricane. I will always be there. You must choose whether you want a fellow preacher … or a thorn in your side."

I am sure that those fellow students in high school who called me names and mocked my rickety thin physique would not connect that "Dead Man" with the man I am today. Indeed, one of them at thirty years of age accepted Christ at one of the many crusades we held in the River Plate stadium without realizing that he once sat on the bench next to that night's preacher.

"I once knew a Gebel in high school," he told his wife later that night. "He had the same name as this Dante Gebel, the youth pastor, but the one I knew was an idiot."

Don't blame him. When you are not popular and they have destroyed your self-esteem, the only reminder is a yellowing photo in an old school yearbook. That unhappy guy in the last row.

Two weeks after that crusade, when the man realized that the idiot from high school and the youth pastor who had preached to sixty thousand young people and introduced him to Christ at the crusade were the same person, he felt like one of Joseph's brothers.

Now, stop for a minute.

Maybe I did not express myself clearly:

I did not ask for a little bit of your attention, I want it all.

Watch me carefully.

Roofer.

Slave.

Self-conscious.

Imprisoned in the dark cell of a complex.

Sentenced by the bony finger of a merciless leader.

I want you to understand what I am about to say. Close your fist and get a grip because you are going to change your inheritance. You remind me of myself when I was fifteen years old; I did not tell you to close your hand halfway, I told you to make a fist so firmly that you can almost feel your fingernails digging into the palms of your hands. Whether you are fifteen years old … or fifty.

Never forget these words: You have the heart of a nobleman. You possess the sacred flame. The sword of the Great King rests on your right shoulder and will change your future forever.

Now, hear the words of the King.

One by one.

Ingest them. Internalize them.

Memorize them always.

Transform them into your theme song, your shield of nobility.

You can change your star.

CHAPTER

2

THE BIG LEAGUES

He has been a thief his whole life. Most criminals have codes regarding which people they should never rob. But he is ignorant of any codes. He was first placed in a juvenile detention center at the age of seven and later he would spend time in all of the city's correctional facilities. Someone who was well acquainted with that kind of people predicted that this little boy would never become an honest adult and he was not wrong. Perhaps there are people born with bad character, a certain kind of karma, something that predisposes them to evil before they reach adulthood. This, ladies and gentlemen, is typically the case. This boy whose parents were unknown had even less hope that anyone would consider adopting him. It was said throughout the neighborhood of his birth that he had already killed ten people. Others thought the number much higher. Everyone knows this, but no one could ever prove anything. They say that after the age of thirty he joined the mafia, gaining a larger network of important friends and influential powerbrokers. And perhaps for this reason, he was never convicted of any crime. Everyone knows that he is a thief; any neighbor will tell you that he is not unaware of the Mafioso that his own city produced. Everyone from the mayor to the judge knows that his business affairs are questionable: drugs, stolen merchandise, white slavery. But his ties to the rich and powerful allow him to act with impunity. He mocks the judges and lives out a turbulent lifestyle openly in the stunned sight of innocent citizens.

But then power changed hands. Perhaps some political deals left him on the losing end, or else an honest judge would not put a price tag on his duty to mete out justice. It has been a year since he lost his freedom. The local newspaper celebrated his conviction with a front-page story in the Sunday paper. The local citizens breathed a sigh of relief that justice was done. Justice was very late, but there was justice at last. Politicians used this Mafioso's imprisonment to strengthen their own campaigns. One influential powerbroker discussed it on local television to show "how justice is working in our city." If there ever were a minute, hypothetical chance that some prisoner would be set free, it would not be him. It is likely that not a single good citizen of that town was unhappy about the just imprisonment of this otherwise obscure person. Those who had been afraid had spoken. And a willing magistrate was able to prove each and every charge of wrongdoing. They also say that no attorney was able to defend the indefensible. He was given a life sentence.

But all that had happened one year earlier. The first twelve months of the rest of his life in prison. Today is a festive day in the city and the custom is to give a "gift." An ironic gift. On this day of celebration, the people can vote that the governor release a prisoner, perhaps to give him a second chance. But this nefarious criminal dares not even dream that he could ever see his own wish fulfilled. The people hate him too much. The people would rise up against the government like hungry lions. No. The possibility of freedom does not exist for him … unless … there were someone in the prison more hated by the people than himself. A child molester perhaps. Or a thief even more unscrupulous than himself. A cannibal, a beast who preys on the elderly, a Hitler, a scourge originating in hell itself. If there were such a person, then perhaps by means of comparisons, the Mafioso could gain the desired pardon and once again freely walk the streets of the city. But for this man such illusions are useless, there is no one worse than himself and he knows it. Suddenly, someone interrupts his thoughts. It is a guard. Surely the guard has come to throw him in the pit of solitary confinement or to beat him until he almost bleeds to death. After all, that has been the routine throughout his infernal year in prison. But he notices that the guard does not look disgusted.

"I do not understand this country anymore," the guard says. "These accursed people have voted to set you free and to imprison another man in your place."

The infamous thief cannot believe what he has just heard: The people have voted to free him. Something is not right – either the whole country has gone crazy or else someone has appeared who is more hated by the people than himself.

Another two guards hand him some street clothes to wear. A scribe confirms his signature in the book that lists inmates released from prison.

It is a moment too miraculous, too unreal for just another afternoon. It is counterintuitive. The man condemned to life in prison has been set free thanks to the same people who had him locked away.

Outside waiting are the journalists, the cameras, the microphones, and the reporters who push and shove each other for a better position. The thief walks out onto the street and immediately the microphones target him. They all want to hear his reaction. They need at least a word or two from him, a statement. But all the thief can do is ask a question. He should answer, but instead he asks. He wants to know who is the monster that will be punished in his place. He wants at least to know the name of the beast who took his place in the lottery of death.

"Jesus of Nazareth," responds an anchorman from a local news station. "The people preferred to have you released rather than that Jesus." The thief does not understand much, and he makes his way through the crowd. He has too many questions to ask, and leaves his interrogators unanswered. He is free, but for some strange reason he is not enjoying the freedom. He does not understand what is happening. This Jesus must have been someone very important to take his place or crazy enough to earn the hatred of the entire city. Perhaps he had few powerful connections or, who knows, maybe it is someone who is making history. The thief stops in the middle of nowhere and he only has one desire, a longing as powerful as that for freedom. The thief wants to meet the person who took his place. He wants to know who has taken upon himself so much hatred. He wants to know who has given him, indirectly, his freedom and a second chance in life. As a matter of fact, over the next two thousand years, everyone will be asking the same question. Everyone will want to know who is this man. Millions of people everywhere will be asking why this Jesus was willing to bear the sins of the world. Why did He take the place of thieves? He is the divine enigma. He is true love. He is the unexplainable Son of God. Everyone will want to ask Jesus: "Why?" But for now, the first person to ask that question might well have been a thief who has been unjustly given his freedom as if by the hand of divine intervention.

FROM SPECTATOR TO STAR

I am certain that you thought you had nothing in common with Barabbas, until you saw him this way. You are only a spectator watching someone else's accomplishments. You don't play in the game; you only buy tickets so that you can watch the game comfortably from the stands.

"*The Gold Cup is a pleasure reserved for winners,*" you think.

You never take a bow to acknowledge the cheers of the spectators. You are among those who applaud. No one ever wants to take your photo. You are the one who buys the newspaper to see how the team champions look.

No one ever asks for your public statement, you are never the subject of news stories, and no one ever requests your autograph. You are just part of the crowd of people watching. At most, you shout when goals are made and freely offer your opinion to anyone who will listen:

"I don't like the coach."

"These seats are not very comfortable and it is cold."

"The referee just made a horrible call."

"They should not have kicked out that player."

"They should have taken the other guy out of the game."

"The championship match is too long, and I don't like the way this game is being played."

"I recently read a book about soccer and I think I know more than the technical director."

"I almost feel like a member of the team. My parents have been bringing me to these games ever since I was a child."

But deep down you know that you could never be on this team. Even if they randomly selected a team member from the crowd, there would only be a remote possibility, perhaps one hundred thousand to one, that it would be you.

So you tell yourself that you were only born to watch and state your opinions. You listen to great sermons delivered by others and delight to hear testimonies of others who serve as role models. But you are not on the reserve team. You are not even second-string. You have dedicated your life to watching games and cheering the champion.

And then it happens.

A world championship game. You buy your ticket and you

find a place where you can see the entire stadium. The team runs out onto the field. It is going to be a great game, broadcast around the world. The flash of cameras transforms the stadium into a virtual electric storm. And then the technical director stops, turns around and searches the crowd. There are one hundred thousand people filling the huge stadium to the brim. The coach whispers into the ear of his star player, the center of the team, number ten. The player begins to climb the steps of the stadium, pressing through the crowds of people who greet him.

You do not understand what is happening. The crowd boos at the coach for delaying the start of the game, while the team's star player climbs higher into the stadium stands. He is getting closer to you and he almost seems to be searching for you.

"There is no way that this could be happening," you think. "It must be a bad joke, a hidden camera prank for the Saturday show."

Now, the leader of the team, the multimillionaire player, the star of the evening is standing before you, completely exhausted.

"The coach wants you to take my place," he says.

"That I what?"

"He wants you to replace me, to take my place."

"You must be mistaken. I am only a spectator. I only came to watch the game," I explain.

"Please don't delay the game. I will watch from your seat; you must go down and play."

"But, I only…well, you are…I only came to…"

Now the crowd is very angry. One hundred thousand spectators are observing this conversation from every vantage point in the stadium. The boos are deafening. The coach is standing motionless in the middle of the field, awaiting your decision.

"Please, go down to the field. You are on the team. This is a strategic change from the coach. Do not delay the championship," the best player in the world says as he sits down in my seat and hands me his shirt.

Does this seem like an irrational story? Interview Barabbas and ask him how he felt when the Champion took his place. We do not know what happened later to this infamous thief or whether he ever played on the great team. But I am sure about what he felt when Jesus took his place. You never forget that day.

You can forget where God placed you, but you never forget from what He rescued you.

YOU ARE A THIEF. YOU ARE NOT ALLOWED TO ENTER THAT SHOPPING CENTER. WHAT YOU DID WAS DISASTROUS.

No, they are not talking about Barabbas. Fast forward to the year 1990. You are pointing at me.

I was the youngest sales manager in the business, but something got in my way. I was absolutely certain that I could never serve God. I lacked character, a healthy self-esteem, and determination. But I was committed to becoming a salesman.

I strove to be the best, but I was a disaster as an administrator. As soon as I was in charge of my own business, I knew that I was not capable of leading people or handling money. One night, the general manager did an inventory and realized that a lot of valuable merchandise was missing. Yelling. Threats. Accusations were exchanged among the employees and telegrams were sent firing everyone, including me. They even restricted my entrance to the store where I worked, calling me a "dangerous individual" and a thief.

At times like these you become firmly convinced that you

can only be a spectator in matters related to God. If you could not even qualify as a simple salesman, forget about dreaming about doing God's work. You buy your ticket and sit back to watch the game. You read books and feast on the experiences of others. The idea that someone someday may single you out seems like a fantasy, a fable.

But the Coach has decided to use you. He has invited you to join the team. You were just part of the group, but now you are unique. You were lost in the crowd, but now you have a name. You were cloaked in anonymity, but now you wear the official shirt of the championship team. You no longer carry binoculars, you now experience the game up close and personal. You no longer snap photographs or ask for autographs. Your mind is focused on winning gold cups and medals.

Do you remember the coach's words when he invited you to join the big leagues? If He has not called you yet, just wait. When He does, record His words. I still remember what He said to me. It is something I will never forget. I was in San Nicolas, a beautiful city in the outskirts of Buenos Aires.

"Dante, you can't go back. I have chosen you to preach to thousands of my young people. They will call you 'Youth Pastor' and 'Evangelist of the new century.' All of your dreams will follow you and will be fulfilled one by one. The day you stop dreaming is the day you stop growing. Believe it or not, I gave you this ministry. You will tirelessly go to the nations, you will go out and return."

When someone reminds you that you are a thief, mention the words of the Coach. When someone shows you a yellowed photograph that reveals your self-conscious past, repeat the words of the coach. It doesn't matter that you have never played or that you are more accustomed to being a spectator. First you must convince yourself that you can change your star. Then you only need to wait for the call to play in the big leagues. The rest is training, hard work, and getting used to winning.

CHAPTER

3

THE CHAMPION'S FIST

Seized by a fit of passion, a man proposes marriage and hopes that he has found true love. Another man dedicates himself to his true career and vocational goal: medicine. A woman leaves behind the distractions of life to attend a Bible seminary in order to prepare for work in some remote corner of the world. A teenager decides to become the best soccer player and, starting now, commits to working as hard as he can to accomplish this goal. Two spouses finally agree that she should not have an abortion and that they will have this child. All of these people have something in common: they have made fundamental decisions that may seem simple but will profoundly affect their own future and, indirectly, the futures of many other people as well.

The first will no longer be a bachelor who needs only worry about what pants he will wear on Saturday. He will become the leader of a family. Another man will save hundreds of lives in the emergency room of a hospital. The woman who decided to go to seminary is now preaching in New Guinea. The young boy is now a well-known soccer star and has just signed a million-dollar contract to play in Italy. The man and wife who decided against abortion now listen to their son giving a presidential speech from the White House. Decisions that cause a cosmic shift somewhere in the world. Decisions that will affect generations to come. Small decisions that may go unnoticed by journalists who record major events but that, with the passing of time, become part of a larger history.

I know of one such story that speaks of simple yet transcendental decisions.

It was a cold morning in May and the man was living through one of the saddest birthdays of his life. He had lived through the first five decades of his life and the future looked bleak. His wife had been ill for several years. It did not matter how many years, the time just seemed like eternity. The man, a carpenter by trade, had watched as the cancer gradually progressed, slowly stealing the life of his dear companion. It was a humiliating disease. When was the last time this man of coarse hands had slept through the night? He hardly could remember. Everything had turned to gray since the awful cancer had entered their lives. His wife did not look anything like the woman in that old wedding portrait hanging on one of their bedroom walls. Now her face looked pale and cadaverous, colorless and thinner than a living person, almost skeletal.

"You are a grown woman," the doctor had said. "Go home and … wait."

The man, though he was temperamental and working class, knew what to expect. The inevitable. The cancer would eventually take his wife and the mother of their four children. Without pity. Without granting a few more years of grace. The stench of death seemed to fill the house as the days passed. Alcohol served as anesthesia for the old carpenter. At least he did not have to think for a few hours. Whenever he was drunk, he found a few moments of respite from his troubles. Bottles of alcohol of every kind could be found all over the house — in the closets, the refrigerator, the garage, the shed, and even hidden in the sawdust of a moldy old barrel. This was his birthday. The man celebrated one more year of life and the loss of another year of his wife's health.

The cries of his wife roused him from his lethargy.

"Remember," she said softly, "that today we are invited to attend that church."

The man grimaced. He had been a Lutheran from childhood but had not set foot in a church for many years. He barely remembered a few religious songs in the German language that were sung in the country of his birth. But his wife's request was not optional. It was a desperate plea. Perhaps this would be the last dying wish of someone who was fighting desperately against an invasive, incurable tumor. Perhaps this would be her last chance to get close to God before leaving this life. The carpenter with coarse hands and alcohol on his breath nodded his head. The church was not close, but when cancer strikes a home, people stop caring about time and distance. No one sleeps in the carpenter's house.

That night, on the man's birthday, the couple arrived with their two youngest children at a church in the remote town of Del Viso, located in the immense Buenos Aires metropolitan area. Those who saw him that night say that he leaned against the wall at the back of the church and listened to the sermon.

"Great way to celebrate his birthday," he must have been thinking, ironically.

But he remained standing there out of respect, watching as his wife cried at the altar. He hardly heard the sermon, but he felt that he needed to be with his wife. Slowly, the man who was hiding bottles of alcohol all over his home went forward. Both of them made a decision that night. They accepted Christ as their only and sufficient Savior. It was a simple decision that did not seem to be of historic proportions at the time and I am sure that very few people there even noticed the carpenter and his sick wife. But their lives were changed forever.

She watched as the cancer receded from her body little by little until it miraculously became just a bad memory. He threw away all of his bottles of alcohol and never drank again. What started out as a bad day ended with a decision that changed their future.

Returning home, the old carpenter went outside to his shed and raised his fist to the air. He was now determined to make a radical change. This was not just any fist raised in a rickety old shed – it is the raised fist of a champion. He will never drink again. He will never leave God. It is a promise. A decision.

This all happened on the first of May of 1975. The carpenter with the calloused hands could never have imagined that his determination would affect not only his family but also thousands of people all around the world. His youngest son, who was at that time only seven years old, now preaches to hundreds of young people all over the world and, among other things, he is writing this book.

A FINAL ASSAULT

Do you remember the young boy who had the heart of a champion? You can always change your star if you are determined. The Lord can call you to play in the big leagues, but if you cannot make decisions, your life will be marked by mediocrity. He may desire that you become a champion, but He will not make it happen.

The glamour of the dream ends at the moment you sign the contract. Then you cannot just stand there watching the burning bush forever. Over the course of my ministry, I have seen many people who had visions, who became drunk on great dreams, but who lacked determination and were never able to realize their dreams.

I know what you are thinking: "Well, if I knew for sure that God had spoken to me or that He had sent me to do a certain job; I would not hesitate for a second to do what He asks."

I thought the same thing until it came time for me to sign my name to a million dollar contract. When I was twenty-four years old, I rented the city's big stadium to hold a crusade. Even though it was only a dream, I was enthusiastic, energized. But when the owner of the stadium stared at me as if I were an insect and said, "Are you aware that the cost of renting the stadium is sixty thousand dollars for one night and that you must pay in advance?"

That is exactly when, for reasons of common sense, you feel like leaving the planet. You do not have money, no one knows who you are, you do not have any financial backing, you are alone; but you must make a decision. This is a decision that may affect the lives of thousands of people and yet your only support thus far is the burning bush you alone saw in the wilderness.

Make yourself comfortable, because I want to tell you a few secrets that are rarely spoken of; I am committed to hiding nothing from you.

During 1998, our ministry was involved in negotiations with the government of the city of Buenos Aires. We wanted to hold a great crusade in the Plaza de la República, a site that is best known for its massive obelisk. Until that time, no one had ever held a massive gathering of Christians in the center of the city. We were sure that God had given us the command, but we had not yet received official permission from the city.

At that time, we were producing a weekly television program broadcast Saturdays on the national channel. We began announcing that we would be holding a great crusade, a mega-event, in the heart of Buenos Aires near the obelisk. We printed thousands of fliers that were distributed all over the country and we promoted the event on all of the radio stations in the country. A few days later, we were seated in the office of one of the representatives of the governor at that time, Dr. Fernando de la Rua.

"Let me see if we understand each other, Gebel," the man said while glancing at me over his glasses. "You cannot promote a huge mega-event at the obelisk of the city center unless you have received our permission. Is that clear?"

The man was upset. You could sense the tension in the air. His desk was immense, and a huge bookshelf weighted with heavy legal tomes lent the office a cold, impersonal feeling. He was smoking a smelly cigar and every once in a while he would reach over and tap it on the large ashtray on his desk flanked by photographs of himself posing with various famous dignitaries of the country.

"This city has an owner," he said in a harsh tone, "and you, young man, cannot hold a large event there. We cannot permit the huge traffic jams, the closed off streets and the possibility of disorderly conduct."

"I understand perfectly what you are saying," I replied calmly, "but we have already publicized the event all over the country. I don't think that we can stop the hundreds of young people who will be arriving by bus from several cities."

I wanted to explain that, in addition, God had told me to hold the crusade — that I was obeying divine orders, that it was a decision that could not be revoked, but the government official was in a hurry and short of words. Therefore, I decided to wait patiently for his answer. The man paused for what seemed an eternity, exhaling thick tobacco smoke that filled the room without relief, intoxicating the chilly room. Then he chose to underestimate.

"If we do grant the official permission you are requesting,

how many young people do you think will gather at the obelisk?"

"More than eighty thousand," I answered, smiling.

"Don't be discouraged, but the only person who ever drew that many people here was named Ricky Martin and, as far as I know, you cannot sing. Put yourself in my place. If I give you permission to hold this event, cordon off the streets, appoint policemen to patrol the area, allow chaos in the city center, and then only your mother and grandmother turn out to hear you speak, then I will lose my job. Do you understand me, Gebel?

Now, I want you to stop simply reading this book and accompany me to that office. Imagine that you are sitting there with me, dizzied by the smoke and chilled to the bone. This man looking at us over his glasses through a cloud of cigar smoke is not joking. This is not your church leader trying to discourage you from holding a youth group meeting this coming Saturday. This is not your wife telling you that she will not have time to make dinner. Neither is this your boss telling you that he cannot give you a pay raise. This man represents the government and everything that he is saying makes sense from a common sense point of view. If he so desires, we will not have the required permission. If he gets angry, he could throw us out of his office and out of a career. And now, he wants us to convince him that we are as popular as Ricky Martin. That eighty thousand young people will show up just because I think they will.

Do you see? I knew you would run away. You want to respectfully get up from your chair and excuse yourself by saying that all of this was a big mistake. We will leave quickly and everything will be forgotten. This is crazy! What were we thinking when we requested this meeting?

But if you want to be a champion, you must have an unbreakable heart. You must have determination. The cost is horrific, but you must try. You cannot turn back now.

At the Olympic Games held in Seoul, Korea, at the end of the one hundred-meter "butterfly" swimming contest, Matt Biondi was favored to win. But he paused to look at the two swimmers in the lanes next to him and, seeing that he was ahead of them, did not extend a final arm stroke. It was a terrible mistake. Anthony Nesty, who Matt could not see, finished first and took the gold medal.

You cannot allow yourself to not make that final effort. One more push, one last round.

"Look, I know that I am not a pop star," I said respectfully, after taking a deep breath — but if you do not give me the permit, instead of an event, there will be a huge demonstration. I cannot control the people. There are only twenty-four days left and believe me when I tell you that we will fill this city."

I do not know what went through his mind, but finally the man smiled or at least tried to smile. Maybe he thought I seemed like a lunatic, or maybe he thought I made sense on some level. He resumed puffing on his cigar for another long while. Finally, he said in an ironic tone: "Okay, this is what we will do. I will do everything possible so that the city government will grant the permit. But even so, if you manage to bring in a minimum of twenty thousand people, only twenty thousand, I will offer you an office and a desk in the government.

This had been a huge victory. And even though the government official was underestimating me, I saw that God had everything in his hands. Within ten days we had the permit that we so desired, and now we had the hard work of actually staging the huge crusade.

Two days before the event, on December 10, an imposing platform was being placed in front of the obelisk in the city center. There were gigantic screens on each side of the stage and an incredible sound system that was contained in huge towers along the main avenue but, no, this was not our event. They were preparing for the "Tango Festival" organized by the cultural secretary, an office that answered directly to the president of the country. A celebration of the tango, the most popular music genre in Argentina, was to take place on the same day, at the same time, and in the same place.

I immediately called my "friend," the government official.

"There must be a mistake," I said, trembling. "You gave me the official permit to hold a crusade for young people at the obelisk, but I have just learned that on the same day, at the same time and in the same place there will be a tango festival."

"That is correct," he said. "You have been caught in the middle of a government battle. We gave you a permit as the independent government of the city, but the tango festival is sponsored by the president himself. I am sorry."

"But, what should I do?" I asked him indignantly. "I can't cancel everything two days before the event."

"Ultimately, that is your decision. If you like, put your platform in front of what is already there. Didn't you say that you could bring more people than Ricky Martin? Come on, Gebel, may the best person win."

It seemed like a bad joke. A joke that was completely out of place. Two platforms side by side with only twenty meters in between. The same starting time for both events on the same day. Two altars. The Gospel and tango. David and Goliath. Baal and Elijah.

This may sound like an epic saga, but I still remember how my wife and I felt – nauseous, heads aching, dizzy, sick to our stomachs. And we were full of questions, many questions. We wanted to hold a crusade, not start a war.

"My counsel is that you call off your event," one pastor said over the phone. "I cannot allow the young people of my church to travel to an event where unpleasant altercations are possible. The Tango Festival was organized by the president of the republic. If I were in your place, I would postpone the event to the near future."

Determination under pressure. Decisions so mortally serious that the future of thousands of people could be affected. Simple decisions that may generate cosmic spiritual results.

During the Olympic games in Sydney, Australia, the American boxer Rulon Gardner decided that he could beat the man favored to win, the Russian Alexandre Kareline. Kareline, also known as King Kong, had not lost a fight in thirteen years. But Gardner won the gold medal.

Misty Hyman, an unknown swimmer, took the title away from Susan O'Neill in the two hundred-meter race. O'Neill held the world record in her specialty until someone decided that she could do better.

Do you remember the old carpenter? Every time I see my father, I remember the day he raised his fist in the air and decided to never drink again. Twenty-seven years have gone by since he made that decision. A champion cannot drop out of the race when there are only one hundred meters to go.

In Munich in 1972, during the ten thousand-meter contest the Swede Lasse Viren tripped and fell. That put the other competitors 50 meters ahead of him but Lasse got up and continued the race. He had not come that far to end in eighth or ninth place, nor could he ask for a second chance. So he did not stay there on the ground – he got up and, running faster than ever, caught up with his competitors. He finished in first place and set a world record: 27 minutes and 38 seconds.

You cannot allow yourself to be intimidated by a rival – even if it is the president himself. If you do not believe me, when you get to heaven ask Moses. Ask him to tell you about Pharaoh and his hardened heart. Ask him about the difference between what he felt standing in front of the burning bush and later, when he confronted the dictatorial ruler of Egypt.

When you receive a vision, you feel like a hero. But when you are carrying out orders and are under pressure, you begin to think that God made a mistake in choosing you.

To finish the story, on December 12, 1998, at nine o'clock at night, we began our crusade at the obelisk and at the same time the tango festival began. They brought in six hundred people – we brought in one hundred thousand. The press was impressed. One of the most important morning newspapers in the country described it this way: "The traditional tango festival was overshadowed by a huge Christian mega-event held to promote family values. They listened to a speaker talking about the need for Argentina to return to God."

We made history that night. One hundred thousand young people filed the main street of the city exalting Jesus Christ for more than four hours. It was one of the biggest spiritual victories of our ministry.

That government official who had underestimated us and would not quit smoking called me one hour before the event to tell me that Dr. Fernando de la Rua would be present at our event. When I reminded him that he had promised me a desk in the government, the only thing I heard was a sheepish laugh. Even so, we received him cordially and prayed for him and the man who was at the time head of the government.

The tango festival lasted barely an hour before they called off the show. We did not have anything against them. It was just that we had the official city permit and they were virtually intruders.

Even though you may not have the funds you need, do not give up. Even when your illness is advancing, do not stop. Even after your heart is broken or you experience a horrible deception, keep on running the race. Do not let your rival underestimate you and keep the title. A last-ditch effort can make the difference between defeat and the gold medal. You can raise the champion's fist up to the sky and make that decision.

Simple determination will always have a lasting effect on many people. And if you still harbor doubts, ask the old carpenter.

CHAPTER

4

THE QUICK WIPE-OUT

His wife had told him before he left the house that this would not be a good day.

It was a strange intuition that had been going around in her head for weeks. Her husband had lived with danger for a long time and death was common currency in his life of dissipation and vice. Each day might be the last time she would see him alive. But this day, the feeling was different.

She had a sense of foreboding, a chilling premonition.

And now the ringing of the telephone dispelled any doubts.

"Mrs. Lopez?"

"Speaking."

"I am calling for the city courthouse. I am sorry to inform

you that your husband, Héctor López, was arrested this morning while he was trying to rob the Central Bank." The man on the telephone did not pause. "You know how the law works in our country. Because this is a second offense he will not have the right to appeal for another hearing or even to petition for another judge. He will be sentenced this very afternoon."

The woman drops the telephone and a chill runs through her body. She feels like her knees are buckling.

"You should have never married him. He was never a good man," her mother had often said and today she was paying the price for a bad decision – for not listening to her mother's counsel. Still, the fact that he was a delinquent did not diminish her love for him. She would have preferred an attorney, an engineer or even a bricklayer, but she did not have that good fortune. Her husband is a thief and the government has all the proof necessary to put him away.

It would come as no surprise to her that he might lose his liberty. She had gone through this before. The frightening thing was that this time the judge would show no mercy and his sentence could not be appealed.

"I am asking that the fullest extent of the law be carried out in this case with an immediate death penalty," the prosecuting attorney might have said in a courtroom filled with witnesses thirsty for justice. "Yes, I knew this was not going to be a good day," the woman thought again and again. "He should never have gotten out of bed this morning."

The sky was cloudy and overcast that afternoon, with a drizzling rain that stung the face.

"Maybe his evil companions were his undoing," she thought as she walked down the main street.

"His accomplice in the robberies was also arrested today at the scene of the crime and will die along with your husband," a neighbor woman said, attempting to console her with this disgraceful news. Nevertheless, there was no reason to look for any other guilty parties. The only thing certain was that her husband's life would end the way she had dreamed in so many nightmares. He would die in the most awful way, the most shameful, the cruelest, the most atrocious, by public execution. The woman never had a chance to say good-bye to her loved one because thieves cannot count on that sort of luxury. No pity, no humanity, no last wish is granted to those who are sentenced to death.

The woman makes her way through a crowd of people clamoring for justice. The people are agitated, riled up. For many, today is a great day for justice. The thieves will pay for their crimes.

On the horizon she sees three crosses outlined against the cloudy sky – there is one for her husband, one for his accomplice, and one for a man who is unknown to her. She recognizes her husband and his accomplice, but she does not see the significance of the third man.

"Perhaps just another unlucky soul who leaves behind another widow and her orphaned children to a life of oblivion and disgrace," she thinks. The sight was shocking but one cannot blame her for not crying now. All of her tears have been shed during a miserable life with someone who promised his undying love but who now hangs on a cross. Screams, pleas, whiplashes, blood, anger. She does not want to look at her husband. He is there, but she prefers not to remember him that way. She only stares down at the dry ground as blood swirls around her feet.

One of the thieves, her husband's accomplice, insults the unknown man whose cross is in the center, between the two thieves. Then she hears a familiar voice speaking barely loud enough to be heard, saying angrily: "Don't you fear God, you who are under the same death sentence?"

The woman is stunned. Her husband has just spoken out in defense of the other delinquent. This is ridiculous, especially when you remember that he often lived by the philosophy that: "One should never get involved in other people's lives. Each person must learn to fend for himself."

That is why she is puzzled. Her husband has never defended anyone or pledged anything on behalf of strangers. "This world is a selfish place," he was wont to say when he was drinking.

"Remember me when you come into your kingdom," he says now.

It was undoubtedly the voice of her husband pleading with the unknown man on the center cross.

"Today you will be with me in paradise," the other man promised, as if he were in any condition to fulfill any promises.

When you are hanging on a cross you beg for mercy, you do not promise paradise, the woman is thinking.

She lifts up her eyes for the first time. Perhaps to look into her husband's eyes one more time or to comprehend the odd conversation she has just overheard. Her husband's accomplice continues to curse the man. The unknown man in the center seems to be an innocent victim who is being punished for something he never did but he also must be crazy to promise a paradise and her husband, *her husband* ... is smilng. There is no reason for him to be smiling, no reason at all. His own life was a miserable existence and now he is hanging on a cross in front of thousands of enraged citizens. But Héctor López meets his wife's gaze and manages a feeble smile, a final gesture signifying that all is well in spite of everything. It is the look of someone who has encountered grace when least expected. She does not understand why, but she senses that her husband has finally found something different. She did not fully understand the conversation between the condemned men, but she knew that something had changed there, only a few yards away from where she stood, up there on the cross.

Her husband is suspended on a cross of wood, but for some unexplainable, irrational reason he is smiling. She returns his look in meaningful silence – a look understood only by those who love each other so deeply that there is no longer any need for words. Her husband has found grace in his final moments. It is perhaps only a matter of seconds before his appointment with the grim reaper, with death. She knows that she has no reason to plead for justice, much less, for mercy. She knows that her husband must pay for the crimes he has committed. She is aware that this is the end of the road for him, the final chapter, whether it comes too early or too late. But now, this last smile on her husband's face has a calming effect. Strangely, the smile that can be seen despite all the bleeding wounds and bruises is reward enough for a whole lifetime of misery.

Her husband hardly appears to be hanging on the cross. In dying he almost seems like an old man lying on his warm bed at home surrounded by his loved ones after having lived a very long, good life. The man did not deserve grandchildren or a long life or a Christian burial or an elaborate tombstone. But someone, a condemned man like himself, has extended the promise of paradise from the heights of a cross. No, earlier that morning she had suspected this would not be a good day. And much less now did she believe there was any possibility that things would end well. Héctor has stopped breathing, but no one can explain why he is still smiling.

The woman does not understand anything about theology, paradise or redeemers. She only knows that something miraculous has just occurred. She has discovered the secret: If in order to find paradise one must come to the cross, coming to this place was worth the effort.

Now I want you to answer a few questions.

How many praise choruses had Héctor learned?

How many times did he hear a sermon?

What credentials did he have?

What was his calling?

And what can you tell me about his ministry? Did he have one?

Did you answer the way I suspected? Let me add just one more thing – you will find Héctor in heaven alongside Moses, David, and the Apostle Paul.

Ladies and gentlemen, this is "grace." The word comes from the Greek "caris" which means "the divine influence in the heart of man." It is the unmerited favor of God towards each one of us. Grace is something we did not earn by our own merits. It is a gift. You were hanging on a cross, but they surprised you with a passport to heaven. You were relegated to the audience, but now they invited you to play in the championship game. Beggars who are turned into princes. Unknown people who leave a mark on history. Anonymous people who are inducted into the Hall of Fame.

THAT HIDDEN WEAKNESS

I still remember the first time it happened. It was at a leadership conference in beautiful Sydney, Australia. The meeting was a true revival, or at least it seemed that way. My job was to preach an inspiring sermon to end the service. The people were loudly clapping their hands and jumping around as the musicians played incredible music. Australian worship is truly amazing.

The ministers in charge of the conference kept asking the people if they were ready to conquer the nation, while the crowd never stopped screaming ecstatically. Are you a preacher? Then you would understand what I was feeling in that instant. It is easier to preach to a group of sinners than to surprise with a fresh word people who already seem to have everything. The young people would not stop dancing and jumping between the chairs of this enormous building. The older people, without exception, were shaking noisy tambourines all over the church. It was what I call a deafening clamour. You either sing and scream, or leave. There is no middle ground.

My dilemma was which message should I give them. These people were almost walking two inches off the floor. During the last song, I switched my outlines and prepared to give them a sermon on encouragement – something about conquest or victory or something like that.

But when everyone was finally seated, something started to happen. While the people watched and waited for me to greet them, I could feel the Holy Spirit whispering to me:

"Talk to them about my grace."

Immediately an intense spiritual battle raged within me. Obviously, God must have been tied up at one of Billy Graham's huge crusades and arrived late to this meeting. Perhaps that explains why He does not know these people very well. I had been there for the whole service. These Australians are experiencing a great revival and they wanted someone to speak to them about things to come, about the ministries of the church, and about the spiritual gifts. They already are forgiven. They are more than sheep – they are first-class leaders. "Tell them that my grace is sufficient for them," the Holy Spirit insisted.

And that is when it happened. I would not have done it if I had not been certain that God was working.

"I want anyone who is involved in a struggle with a hidden sinful addiction to confess it tonight. I am referring to the "giant" that beats you down in private. Perhaps no one suspects it, not even your wife, your parents, or your best friend, but you know that this hidden 'habit' is ruining your anointing."

The silence in the building was deafening.

"You know that you should have an anointed ministry, but you settle for much less because of this weakness that gives you no relief. It does not matter how holy you look when you know that this addiction makes your anointing impure."

God knows that I had only spoken a few words when someone in the crowd broke the silence with heaving sobs.

"I want everyone to close their eyes," I said, "and I want those people who are taping this event to turn off their cameras and recorders. I do not want anyone to be embarrassed. I am asking you, if you realize that your stupid habit is the thing that is keeping you tied to the past and mortgaging your future, to raise your hand."

A few hands, maybe ten or twelve, timidly went up.

"Be more specific," the Holy Spirit told me in a clear voice.

"I am talking about those who cannot stop compulsive masturbation, and those who are addicted to Internet pornography, magazines or any other form of pornography. Those who virtually wake up in a stranger's bed, deceiving their wives in their minds. Those who wish their wife would die, a sudden accident, so that they would be widowed and free to marry another woman they already have in mind. Those who are consumed relentlessly by impure and lustful thoughts. Those who have allowed themselves to engage in fondling of genitals and perhaps even premarital sex with their girlfriends. Those who struggle with homosexual thoughts."

Now the whole building was full of raised hands. The leaders, the sponsors, and even those who moments earlier were ready to conquer the nation. There they were, crying bitterly, discouraged at asking forgiveness over and over again for the same chronic sin.

The first time that you sin, you prostrate yourself in the presence of God and plead for mercy, praying that the blood of Christ will make you clean and pure again. The second time you sin, you think you need to promise something, repeat a phrase like "I promise never to do this again" or "I will never again look at pornography or entertain those impure thoughts." The third time, you impose on yourself a penalty, something that will cause pain, to show God that this time you are serious: "I am going to cancel my cable television service" or "I will start going to the post office again instead of using my email account so that I will not be tempted to visit pornographic sites," or "I will leave my boyfriend even though I think that I love him."

The fourth time, you no longer want to go. Now you really

feel like your life is a fraud. It is one thing to make a mistake one, two, even three times. But now you have lost count." You say to yourself: "I think that God is sick and tired of watching me mess up."

"Do not doubt it," replies the voice of the one who wants to ruin your life. "You have a problem, a weakness, a horrible and repugnant sin that puts you out of the game. Masturbation is your kryptonite — it is destroying you. If I were in your place, I would distance myself from holy things because they obviously are not for people like you."

It is then that a counterintuitive feeling, something irrational, comes upon you. You postpone prayer until after you are cured of your weakness. You set aside all things holy because you feel unworthy, dirty. You do not get involved because you believe that you have gone beyond the limits of forgiveness. And you convince yourself that you were not born to be a champion. Your addiction has left you on the sidelines, only partway toward the finish line, fallen face down on the racetrack.

I asked one last question that night in Sydney. How many of you feel like God does no longer want to forgive you?

I believe that absolutely all the people raised their trembling hands. The same people who seemed to be living out a great revival of healing were now confessing their own sense of being unworthy of God.

I do not want you to misinterpret my words. I am not trying to make excuses for sin. I consider myself to be one of the greatest defenders of holiness. For many years I have dedicated my ministry to preaching about integrity. The theme of our crusades has been to proclaim a holy generation. But holiness without grace is only legalism.

Those thousands of leaders were so mistaken. They had lived with their weaknesses for so long that they no longer believed that God would be willing to even listen to their prayers. Hidden addictions have a unique way of putting you outside the door of the temple, like the lame man who is left begging at the gate of the Beautiful Temple.

You have a lameness that hinders you from walking. Your prayer life has dwindled to a mindless repetition of two or three meaningless sentences before falling asleep. Your communion with God is nonexistent. You are standing at the door – you know everything that goes on inside the church, but you also know what is happening outside. You live in the middle as any nominal Christian would. You know too much to be considered an unbeliever, but not enough to be regarded a saint. You live holy sometimes, but you also sin a little. You worship God and you also speak curses sometimes. You lift your eyes to the heavens at times, but on certain occasions you have wandering eyes.

You have a lame soul. You are spiritually disabled. Your ministry is crippled. Your heart is paralyzed by a stupid hidden addiction. You have the horrible feeling that God no longer wants to see you.

"I am sorry," the angel seems to be saying by way of excuse. "I told God that you came to see Him, but He tells me that you are too worldly to come here."

George Best was declared the best soccer player in all of Europe for 1968. The sports writers all said that he had everything – style, intelligence, control of the ball, physical conditioning, professionalism. It was said that he might possibly be the best soccer player of all time. Nevertheless, a hidden habit destroyed him. He never became all that he could have become. George was a chronic alcoholic and the bars in London were under orders not to serve him alcoholic beverages because drinks could kill him.

What was hidden ruined his public reputation.

If you feel the sting of your own sinfulness and you believe that it is already too late, then remember Héctor López hanging on the cross. He does not deserve forgiveness but he has the good fortune to encounter the giver of grace.

Are you still not convinced? Then follow along as I introduce you to a king. I am sure that you have heard of him.

He is brave in battle and an excellent administrator. He is a dynamic leader and crusader. He is a musician and is very popular. Surveys place him in first place in the hearts of the people. He is a strategist and deeply loves God. His name is David. And God says that he is a man after God's own heart.

But David lusts after a woman who is not his. She is the wife of another man. He looks at her and his hormones seem to explode. He wants to sleep with her at any cost. He desires her, gives the order, has the candlelight dinner prepared, readies his bedroom and enjoys a night of pleasure. Passionate sex.

In a few days, the woman will notice the signs of pregnancy and she will call the king. She will tell him that she is expecting a child.

"There is no doubt that the baby is yours," the beautiful woman will say.

Then the king will no longer behave like a monarch. He will behave like a beast – full of guilt, fear, and indifference. He will want to avoid a scandal. He will devise a Machiavellian plan. He will send out an entire army, if necessary, to bring this woman's husband away from the battle. And he will tell this man that he wants to "reward" him with a gift. One night of love with his wife. If the soldier accepts this "reward," the woman will never be able to claim that the baby belongs to the king.

But the soldier is an honorable man. He believes that it would be an abuse of privilege for him to go home to sleep with his wife while his comrades in arms are sleeping on the battlefield fighting a war on King David's behalf. Even so, the king invites him for drinks.

The soldier accepts the invitation and, again, the king offers the "reward." And again the king's proposal is rejected by the soldier.

The soldier again camps outside and refuses to sleep in his house, showing that even when drunk and tottering, he still displays more dignity than the king when he is sober.

It is then that the administrator, the psalmist, the anointed one, the man so brave-hearted, conspires to have the man killed. May no one ever find out where this soldier spent the night. The plan is almost perfect – a well-planned crime. An honorable death in the midst of battle. And a man descending to the darkest place in his soul because of hidden sin. First came the desire, then a passion lasting no more than fifteen minutes, the adultery, the lies – all those things that turned him into the mastermind of a deliberate crime.

The prophet Nathan asks for a meeting with the king and unmasks him. The monarch cries and pleads that his anointing not be removed. That the presence of the Almighty not depart from his life. That he would be willing to give up the scepter and the crown in order to regain intimacy with God. And once again, the Giver of grace appears on the scene. David will have to face the consequences of his sin, but his repentance is genuine and this opens the doors of true forgiveness for him. It is a sublime forgiveness, unique, one that will never be forgotten. It is a forgiveness that clears the historical record.

As a well-known speaker once said: "When God forgives, He not only forgets, He forgets what He forgot".

Years later the Giver of grace will talk to David's son, to Solomon, and will tell him to have a perfect heart, to have the integrity of his father. David was still regarded as a man after God's own heart. His sin is no longer recorded in the archives of heaven. Neither does it appear on the hard drive of some celestial computer. It has already been deleted from the "Recycle Bin." God has forgotten. The account was canceled.

I still remember some of the facial expressions of those leaders in Sydney. It was the first time I had preached about grace, and since then I have not ceased to mention it. When they believed that they were out of the big leagues, someone believed in them. The trembling hands of great champions, those who would not go into the ring because they considered themselves cripples. The miracle of grace covering the empty places in the soul. Those shadowy corners of intimacy now saturated by the light of a second chance. God, once again, ready and willing to forgive them, reminding them that "my grace is sufficient for all."

Free sex, pornography, lust, masturbation.

Lies, deceit, adultery.

A stranger's bed, impure thoughts, wandering eyes.

It does not matter what type of sin. The secret is that if, in order to have eternal life, to go to heaven when you die, you have learned that you must first come to the cross, then it was worth getting out of bed this morning.

CHAPTER

5

THE
UNIQUE
SQUADRON

No one can make the sniper perched atop a towering sky-scraper give up without accomplishing his objective. The police stand by helplessly as the scoundrel shouts his demands while aiming at them from one of the highest points in the city. Judges, journalists, photographers, police, and hundreds of onlookers gather around the macabre spectacle. Finally, the old commissioner wipes the sweat off his glasses and speaks. Perhaps these are the words that everyone has been waiting to hear: "There is nothing else we can do. Call in the SWAT team."

A sigh of relief is heard from the crowd of people gathered around the chief of police.

Undoubtedly this is a job for men who are specially trained for such risky missions. In a matter of minutes, the SWAT team takes control of the situation. The men in blue emerge from their vehicles with the precision of eagles. They exchange very few words. There is no nervous yelling, only sparsely worded orders, almost as if each one of them already knows what he must do. They speak using code words; it is a specialized terminology. They surround the building. Two of them climb the stairs to the most dangerous position, the terrace; others stand silently around a building nearby. They do not seem to sweat. Their movements are calculated. These men know the danger because they have studied and are well prepared for just this moment. Above all, they know that their job begins after everyone else has given up.

If they do not accomplish the task, there is no other option. They are the one and only alternative. They are the SWAT team. The squadron trained for the most dangerous emergency situations. Armed resistance to dangerous invaders. The ultimate secret weapon of the police force. They are the men in blue. To conquer or die is their motto. They are lethal and precise. This squadron is specially trained for unique missions.

ANOTHER STORY

The man scales down a wall with the grace of a gazelle. The Soviets are monitoring everything with their sophisticated equipment. But he seems to mock the Russian guards. The danger increases with each step, but the intruder is smiling. His work is extremely dangerous, but he grins like an elf hidden in a thicket in the forest. He knows that he can fly an airplane, parachute from fifteen hundred meters, camouflage himself amidst his enemies, and, of course, carry away all of the Russians' ultra-secret information stored on a tiny microchip.

He is the only one who can accomplish this mission. He was carefully trained to deal with the pressures of extreme danger. He has a license to kill if necessary. His enemies fear him, his colleagues respect him, and his boss trusts him completely. He is Bond, James Bond. Another man trained for special missions. Someone who is only getting started at the point where others have long since given up.

The two stories are similar and they have a common denominator – the mission. It is to conquer or to die in the attempt. That is what the new generation that God is raising up is all about. One last generation of fearless leaders trained for the last and final mission – to bring the entire world to the feet of Jesus Christ. They never retreat. They are always ready for action. They are not seeking after a title or a position of celebrity and human recognition. They know that the one thing that matters is lost souls. While others make excuses or try to argue, they take action. While others ask the enemy for permission or try to negotiate, they simply invade.

This army is not composed of passive people. They are invaders by nature. They invade colleges, preach to the faculty, and stir up entire universities. They upset the nations and revolutionize their cities until every place is filed with Jesus Christ. Hell has placed a price on their heads, but they simply smile because they know for whom they are working. They are not predictable or routine. They only surprise. They are the last squadron called to intervene in dangerous situations. Or better said, they are the workers for the eleventh hour.

People with unique missions. If you have a crowd mentality, you should not even continue reading this book. But I imagine that you desire something more than merely to compete. You thirst for victory. This quality is present in those who are only getting started where others are giving up. You would rather die trying than to be left alone with a vision of what could have been. You are determined to change your destiny, to play in the championship game, to win first place.

I know hundreds of people who have abandoned their dreams because they believed that all of their resources were already exhausted. Instead of feeling like they were part of the SWAT team, they believed they were just ordinary policemen on the fat commissioner's payroll.

"I lost my job."

"When all is said and done, that ministry was not for me."

"Well, I did not want that job anyway."

"At least they almost increased my salary."

"I attended the wedding of the woman of my dreams. She married someone else."

"They told me to leave my information and that they would call me."

"I did everything possible and I do not believe there is any-thing else to do."

"I will be content if only they will make a little place for me."

These are typically statements of those who feel they are

condemned to be just another face in the crowd, just another conformist who would settle for eighth place. Lack of determination. A crowd mentality.

A NEW MOTIVATION

Watch as the Lord approaches the disciples' boat. The disciples are resigned after a long night of fishing. Now they wash their empty nets in silence. A collection of bothersome algae and debris is perhaps the only result of another night of failure.

"Let's go fishing," the Master says.

Now pause for a moment to watch the expressions on the apostles' faces. Watch Peter. He is literally haggard, exhausted.

"You take care of raising the dead, and we will do the fishing," is perhaps the thought in the mind of this man from Capernaum.

But do not think of Peter as rude. The Master's proposal really is crazy. They have already tried all night long. Not for just a few hours, the entire night.

It is one thing to make that kind of proposal to someone who has not already tried and failed, but it is another thing entirely to those who have already done everything that could be done.

Have you ever been in that position? Of course you have.

Remember that morning when you unplugged the telephone so that the bill collectors could not reach you. Perhaps you were expecting an easy miracle after a long night's prayer vigil, but when nothing happened you decided that the best course of action would be to say nothing.

Remember that long and feverish night you spent placing fresh cold cloths on the forehead of your sick child? All night long. Hour after hour until daybreak. Can you remember how you felt when the first rays of sunlight streamed through the window without signifying the end of a well-deserved night of rest?

Or that time you came home empty-handed after spending an entire day looking for work? You were discouraged, deeply anguished. The night before you were hopeful, but now, after having tried everything, you are left with only the chagrin of failure. A bitter taste, a net devoid of fish and filled only with debris.

You did your best on the exam but you failed.

You worked hard but your client did not like your work and hired someone else.

You prepared your best sermon and the congregation did not appreciate it.

You prayed all night and the next morning the sickness of the person you prayed for got worse.

You sent an excellent resume but they buried it underneath a pile of paper.

And now Jesus appears on the bitter shore of your life and tells you to try again.

"Cast the net," He says.

"It seems to me that you do not understand about the night I just experienced. I am exhausted, I feel very tired. I need a little sleep, maybe a refreshing nap, but I definitely do not need to fish."

Now let's see if we understand each other. You are not talking to some vagrant, you are talking to a working man who really has done everything. And when I say everything, I mean everything.

But the Lord insists. He wants you to begin where the others left off. He wants to take away that crowd mentality. He wants you to mock the Soviet guards, to neutralize the sniper on that skyscraper. He wants you to do something unique.

Tomorrow morning go out and look for a job all over again.

Prepare to take the exam again as if you had never failed.

Spend another feverish night at the sickbed knowing that it could be the last.

Go to your creditors once again and beg for another chance.

Cast the net for the umpteenth time.

Remember, just one more round could make the difference.

Peter pauses for a moment and thinks of the benefit. This time the Master will be in the boat. It will be like playing in a World Championship football match with the referee on your side. Then Peter speaks those words. These are the words of people who go the second mile. These are the words of one destined for success. "But on your command, I will cast the net."

The fish almost seem to know who is in the boat and decide that it is better for them to die in the Creator's net than to live without ever having the honor of knowing Him. And now the net is bulging with fish.

Someone tried again after all of his recourses were spent.

Someone was just getting started while other fishermen were already cleaning their nets.

When you are able to convince yourself that you are prepared for unique missions, that is when you will discover the potential of what God can do through you.

I still remember what I felt in February 2000 when the Lord showed me that I should travel the entire length and breadth of my country. It was a crazy idea. Ludicrous.

I knew of others who had attempted this plan but had not been able to complete the mission. Argentina is too large to reach the entire country by land. The idea of doing so lacks even a drop of common sense. Besides, we had already tried this and failed.

"Cast the net," He said.

Immediately afterward the Lord gave me a message, "Spiritual Diagnosis," along with the team that would travel along with me. And the finances we would need began arriving bit by bit, month after month.

Starting in April of that year we visited twenty-two provinces in eight months. We carried along technical equipment, including a sound system and we rented stadiums, paying all of our own expenses.

The idea was ambitious and demanded a huge dose of faith, but it was worth the effort.

We experienced cold weather, snow, extreme heat, rain, and grinding exhaustion. On one occasion we visited four provinces in four days — La Rioja, Catamarca, Tucuman, and Santiago del Estero. Each of these cities has a unique culture. The north is the antithesis of the south. People responded differently to the same program. Argentina is a crucible of races and cultures.

Each stadium was a world apart. The technicians had to set up sound systems in venues ranging from modern auditoriums to barnlike warehouses that had been adapted to serve as amphitheaters. During the first leg of the journey, about ten provinces, we traveled in a bus that someone had kindly loaned us, as well as a huge truck carrying the sound equipment. Later on, someone gave us a newer minibus and other vehicles. A few also traveled by airplane, but most of the forty people on the team traveled the twenty-eight thousand kilometers on the national highways. The men would take turns driving until they were overcome with exhaustion.

No sooner had the national anthem begun playing in the stadium, at the starting time for each crusade, than the exhaustion would disappear. The sight of thousands of young people waiting in the snow for another word, to watch them listening to the spectacle from outside the stadium because the building was already filled to capacity, to listen to them singing for hours, and, above all things, to sense that common denominator that still resounds in my mind: that thirst for a new message from God. Once the program had begun there was only one Argentina, north or south.

Later, the closing event held at the imposing Boca Juniors stadium drew an audience of seventy thousand young people. And they came from all of those distant corners of the country that we had so recently visited.

The people in attendance came from many walks of life. People from the provinces were sitting alongside the city dwellers of Buenos Aires. The devoutly religious and the atheist. But I am certain that at that moment, only for one glorious and unforgettable moment, we were equals. Of course the exhaustion and the financial challenge were worth the effort. In all, two-hundred-and-sixty-thousand young people attended the national tour crusade.

The net bulging with fish.

Beginning where others had given up.

A unique mindest.

Missions that others abandoned.

You can make excuses for your meager finances. Say that you are not prepared. Or say that you are really just waiting on orders from God, for His perfect will, a sentiment that at times is nothing more than laziness disguised as piety for the sake of appearance. No one is requiring you to stand out from the crowd. You are welcome to stay there. Tell Him that you already tried everything. That He should focus on healing lepers while you take tests or search for ministry opportunities. Put yourself under the command of that obese police commissioner and watch while the SWAT team resolves what you never had the courage to do.

Devote the rest of your life to washing nets.

There aren't many options available. The other option is to serve on God's unique squadron.

Their methods are different but they get results. They do not have a crowd mentality. They are unique within their lineage, holding a license to cast out demons.

They belong to a special emergency team in the battle against invading armies.

Spiritual warriors who are always prepared.

The battle strength of a new century.

A squadron to fight in the vanguard.

An armed and dangerous division that sets the rules.

Spiritual giants who only play in the big leagues.

The worst nightmare that hell ever brought upon itself.

An army of untouchables in the service of the General of generals.

Agents of spiritual espionage in the enemy's camp.

A brigade of young people trained to succeed.

A force that is unaware of the meaning of the word "defeat."

The only ones capable of descending to hell itself to conquer the enemy.

Fighters who do not wait for things to happen, but who make things happen.

An army that suddenly takes over the stage.

Soldiers with no margin of error.

Agents with a motto: To evangelize or die in the attempt. Never retreat, never surrender, never.

Fighters on red alert who live in the eye of the hurricane.

A squadron with a theme: For every soul destroyed by the devil, we will reclaim one hundred for Jesus Christ.

There is no third option: You are either unique or you are just lost in a crowd.

CHAPTER

6

DETERMINED, COMMITTED, ENTHUSIASTIC

They have known each other ever since grade school. They are five friends who are friends for life.

Every Friday they get together for pizza even if their only excuse is to see one another again. Three of them are married with children. Anthony is an attorney and has two beautiful daughters. George is a newlywed and his wife is expecting a baby. Richard is the father of four children. Diego is one of the bachelors in the group but those who know him say that it will not be long before he joins the married demographic. He is head-over-heels in love with a redhead he met at his office.

The fifth friend is named Javier. He is … well, he isn't … better said, he does not have a permanent job and he is not married. He cannot do these things because he is crippled. An accident that occurred when he was just five years old changed the course of his life. A drunk driver broke his spinal column and his future.

But this Friday is different. They have not even tasted the pizza; the friends have made a decision.

"They say he is very good and he will be in the city," Diego says.

"It doesn't make any sense," says Javier. "If we go there and nothing happens, then I will just feel worse."

Javier's answer sounds logical. The others' lives will continue as usual, but, when all is said and done, he is the cripple, the paralytic. If this unknown healer were a fraud, instead of feeling better, things would only seem worse.

"We don't lose anything by trying," George insists. "They tell me that he has even raised people from the dead, and he has healed several lepers."

"I have the address of the place where he will be staying tonight," Diego says.

Javier is feeling very uncertain, but there is not much to lose. His friends are determined.

A Friday night is the perfect time for a large crowed to gather around the house where the Master will speak. The people are crammed into the kitchen, sitting on the counters and on top of the refrigerator. Even the border on the chimney serves as seating for a dozen or so people, one on top of another. There are no chairs available. Those who can are seated on the wooden floors. The rest are standing around the window frames or on top of other furniture. Someone is proposing to set up chairs outside. They will not be able to see him outside, but at least they may have the honor of hearing Him.

The five friends arrive late.

"I knew this was going to happen," says Javier. "You could not squeeze a pin in there. Take me home and we can come back another day."

"I don't think the Master is going to be here tomorrow. We must try."

The four friends have something more than hope as they carry their crippled friend. They have determination.

"I'm sorry," says a big guy with the smelly breath of a fisherman who calls himself Peter. "There is no more room here. You should come back another day; besides, the Master has already begun to speak and we cannot interrupt Him in the middle of His message just to accommodate another paralytic."

The excuse offered by the bearded host would be enough to discourage any other moderately intelligent man. But it is not enough to hinder these four friends, those carrying the fifth friend, from pursuing their goal of reaching the Healer. And now, they are not only determined, they are also angry.

"You are the one who does not understand!" Anthony says in a raised voice, pointing with his index finger directly at the coarse fisherman's nose. "We haven't come this far to ask when the next service will be held. Our friend is physically disabled and he must see the Master. Today. Not tomorrow. Now!"

Some of the people who are trying to push their way in are starting to get annoyed. Some bystanders turn and tell the intruders to be quiet, that the distraction is preventing them from hearing the voice of the preacher coming from inside the house. Peter shrugs his shoulders and goes back inside the house, pushing and shoving his way through the tightly packed crowd.

"There is nothing we can do," Javier whispers. "We cannot get in. It is too crowded."

"We will get in," Diego says, glancing at the terrace.

Diego and Anthony clamber up a large fig tree whose branches overhang the house and lands on the roof. George improvises a rope using the blankets that were covering Javier's legs. Richard begins to tie it around the arms and waist of the crippled friend. Determined. Committed. Enthusiastic.

No one is paying much attention to the intruders. They all want to get closer to the Master's voice, to touch him, to take his photograph.

The friends examine the chimney but decide that it is too narrow. Instead they begin to remove roof tiles. Anthony remembers that he always carries a toolbox in his car and he goes back to the parking lot for a handsaw. They must have a meeting with the Master even if, in the process, they must tear apart the roof.

The risk is high. If they break a supporting beam the entire roof could cave in. Or Javier could fall and hurt himself. But they are determined to get inside.

Peter is trying to signal Thaddeus to let him know that intruders are trying to rip a hole in the roof. They are interrupting the Master's sermon. They are distracting the people and ruining a Friday night service.

Now the friends know they have reached the point of no return. They will either quickly finish opening the roof or someone will kick them off the roof by force. The disciples are looking for a ladder to climb onto the roof and teach some manners to these impertinent guests. Bartholomew finds a lantern, but Peter is too impatient to wait for a ladder and begins to climb up the fig tree.

"This is crazy,' says Javier. "We are going to end up on the front page of all the newspapers." He is very frightened.

But his friends are not going to let him think too much. The opening is already big enough to send down the man who urgently needs an encounter with the preacher. They take the ropes and lower their friend. Determined. Committed. Peter arrives in time to points them out with his flashlight. He is very angry but it is already too late. The sermon has been interrupted. The crowd watches, some in stunned silence and others angrily, at the first elevator in recorded history.

The crippled man lands face to face with the Master. The four friends watch from the roof. They did it. Javier is meeting Jesus. The keyboardist tries to distract from the commotion by playing some melody, but the Master tells him that is not necessary. That He is amazed at the faith of these men. He pauses the sermon long enough to forgive the man's sins and to order him to walk.

Now the people who would not let Javier inside are giving him a standing ovation. Javier is still wobbling but he takes his first faltering steps. Someone proposes singing a victory chorus, and the musicians begin to play at this Friday night miracle service.

They say that no one wanted to repair the roof and that it was left as a monument to the determination of five friends. They say that the opening is a reminder to those who give up too easily, that it is never too late if the Lord is still in the house.

Javier recovered the use of his legs because of his faith and because of the determination of his four lifelong friends.

Their decision gave courage to the woman who suffered from a flow of blood. She pushed her way through the crowd to touch the hem of the Creator's garment. Enthusiasm was what encouraged Bartimaeus to continue yelling over the crowd. Determination is a quality of champions, of those who must achieve even if it requires tearing apart a roof or enduring a bitter experience along the way.

In the middle of the eighteenth century, in the offices of an elementary school in a small town in Ohio, in the United States, the following conversation was heard: "The child has a slight mental retardation that hinders his ability to acquire learning at the same level as his classmates. You must stop bringing your child to this school."

The woman did not seem very upset by the teacher's pronouncement. Instead, she made sure to tell her son that he was not retarded and that God, in whom he had faithfully trusted from earliest childhood, had not given him life in order to embarrass or shame him, but to become a man of success, that in spite of the teacher's comment, he could change his destiny.

A few years later that boy at the age of twelve founded a newspaper and began to sell copies at a New York train station.

That was not all. He dedicated himself to studying electricity and, thanks to his determination, was able to perfect the telephone, the microphone, the megaphone and other inventions such as the phonograph, to name only a few.

Everything seemed to be smooth sailing until the day when he encountered a huge obstacle. One of his biggest projects seemed to be falling apart before his eyes. He had searched untiringly for a way to build a filament capable of generating incandescent light while at the same time withstanding the electrical current that produced the light.

His financiers were growing impatient. His competitors seemed like they might find the solution before him, and even his co-workers were getting desperate.

After three years of hard work, one of them decided that tearing apart roofs was not worth the effort. He decided that the paralytic could wait for another time.

"Thomas, forget this project. We have been working on it for more than three years. We have tried it more than two thousand different ways and we have experienced only failure each and every time."

It made sense. Yes, there were now two thousand reasons not to try again. But this man had determination. He looked at his collaborator and said, "Look, I don't know what you call failure, but I am sure of one thing and it is this, that in all this time I have learned that rather than think about two thousand failures I have learned more than two thousand ways not to build this filament and that gives me enough guidance to know that I am on the right track."

A few months later, he lit an entire street using the electric light. His name was Thomas Edison and he possessed the qualities of a winner. His was the stock of those who triumph. The sacred flame of those who have gold medal fever. Determination.

Juan Manuel Fangio was the racetrack driver who won the Formula One World Cup championship more times than anyone else in the history of automotive racing competition. One time someone asked him what his secret was. "In order to win, you must reach the finish line," he answered.

His answer might seem childishly simple, but it encapsulates the determination to achieve in spite of circumstances, to overcome any excuses, to overcome mediocrity.

You can determine to change your destiny and it is even possible that you may be invited to play in the big leagues. Perhaps you will make a major decision, lifting your fist to the sky and fighting hand-to-hand combat with your own weakness. But you will not win unless you are determined.

A FASCINATING LOVE STORY

I still remember the first time I understood what it meant to be firmly committed to something. Determined to die, if necessary. And for that matter, have you ever been in love? Then you must read this story.

It happened during a monumental evangelistic crusade led by the well-known evangelist Carlos Annacondia in the city of San Martin, located in the province of Buenos Aires. The writer of this story, yours truly, was sixteen years old and until that time had not known what it meant to fall in love at first sight.

There were twenty-five thousand people filling that huge open field. It was freezing cold but the preacher and the thousands of people gathered there did not seem to care.

It was then that I saw her.

She was sixteen, or maybe seventeen.

Incredibly beautiful. Her skin was white, very white with only a sprinkling of freckles, a decorative detail that seemed to illuminate her face. When she smiled, two dimples adorned her cheeks. Her jet-black hair delicately brushed against her shoulders. She was extremely thin and yet beautifully shaped. She had perfect measurements. She was wearing a marine-blue skirt, a blouse covered with small polka-dots, and a gray jacket with black polka-dots scattered evenly over the fabric.

She was wearing a small badge that identified her as a crusade worker.

At that time I thought that if Carlos Annacondia has this type of collaborator on his team he must be genuinely anointed by the Almighty.

The beauty of that young woman was overwhelming. I believe that some snowy white doves were flying all around her and crystal bells were ringing harmoniously as the woman of my dreams walked through that immense field.

My heart was beating so hard I thought it would fly out of my chest. I had to meet this angel. I seriously considered pretending to be demon-possessed so that she would notice me, but the risk was too high. I could not expose myself to ridicule without knowing for sure that she would notice me.

On my way home that night I decided to return to that meeting every night until the end of the crusade. My mother thought that a great touch of God was operating in my heart.

I spent thirty-eight days of that long crusade loving her in silence. Each night after the service I would return to my house knowing that tomorrow I would see her again. The sermons of the evangelist had never before seemed so sweet. The praise choruses became the calls of a siren. Every night it seemed almost magical if I could by chance watch her from where I stood in the crowd.

The thirty-ninth day was a rainy Saturday. The crusade had already begun as usual when someone interrupted my ponderings. It was Celina, one of my brother's friends. She greeted me respectfully and tried to start a conversation. To tell the truth, I wasn't interested in talking to anyone. I did not want to lose sight of this woman who had captivated my attention.

Suddenly, Celina looked in the same direction that I was looking. Then the unthinkable happened.

"Liliana!" my neighbor shouted, "Liliana!"

The woman of my dreams was the Liliana she was calling. She slowly turned her head and looked in our direction.

"Do you know her?" I asked intently.

"Oh, of course. She is my classmate at school," Celina said casually.

That day I learned two simple truths:

One: Never underestimate anyone.

Two: Celina was like the Angel Gabriel incarnate in a woman who would plead my case.

Now the beloved one I had only glimpsed from a distance was starting to become a reality. She had a name, Liliana, and she was smiling as she walked toward me and this friend of my soul, the one anointed by the Almighty, Celina. I can close my eyes and remember every second of that journey. As she got closer, she became more and more beautiful. Everything around her seemed to be moving in slow motion. Nothing else mattered. The doves continued to fly around her and the bells now seemed to be clanging wildly.

The two girlfriends greeted each other only inches away from the place where I was standing. I remember praying frantically. This was the chance that I had been awaiting for almost forty days. It was God who had lined up the cosmos and aligned the planets so that destiny would allow this casual encounter.

"Liliana, I want you to meet a friend," said Celina, completely "inspired" by Lord, "Dante Gebel."

That was the moment when I met her. The woman of my dreams, the first woman to conquer my heart, was waiting for me to say something, to make some gesture.

Do not misunderstand me. I had practiced what I would say if by chance my destiny and good fortune allowed me the opportunity to meet her. It needed to be a short but meaningful sentence, incisive, perfectly timed, and overwhelmingly brilliant.

But my nerves got the better of me.

"He....llo," I said in a quivering voice. I turned nervously to look the other way as if I were completely uninterested in her.

Why do we wait our whole lives for a girl to return our interest and then we act as if we don't care?

Why do we spend our whole lives practicing in front of a mirror what we will say and yet when we are standing in front of the girl, we say the first stupid thing that comes out of our mouths?

She, the woman of my dreams, acknowledged my pitiful greeting with a nod and carefully continued chatting with Celina. The writer of this book continued to look in the other direction still trying to think of something witty to say – something moderately intelligent that would put me back in the race. But my brain was too exhausted or too addled.

Liliana, the beautiful one I loved from a distance, said goodbye to her friend and turned around to return to the crusade. She stood only a few inches away from me and all I could muster was a shrill "Hello."

I felt like a failure, a fiasco. I could not yet declare my love to her, but I could have at least said something faintly romantic. Or at least sound intelligent.

Five years went by. Five long years without seeing her again. At the end of 1989 I was in charge of directing the praise choruses and worship for the evangelistic services of a well-known man of God. We visited several congregations and held a series of revival meetings. We arrived at a church where, thanks to one of the musicians, I learned that Liliana was a member. She had not married, had not gained weight or suffered a serious accident, nothing that would cause her teeth to fall out, or lose her hair, or burn her face. I know this sounds frivolous and superficial, but at that time it was very important for me to know whether she had maintained her beauty over those five long years.

This was going to be my second meeting with her after such a long time. I had to find out for myself how I would feel when I saw her again. Was it only an adolescent infatuation or was that feeling of love still there in my soul?

I was leading a song that said: "Take my hands, I ask you; take my lips, I love you; take my life, O Father, I am yours."

It was then that I saw her entering the church. I saw her figure silhouetted in the main entrance to the church. The years had been good to her. She was even more beautiful than I remembered. Her figure was svelte, delicate. There were bells and the doves once again, although a bit older perhaps, but still there fluttering around the princess.

Nothing else was needed. My heart felt like it was about to explode. If it was my destiny to die at that moment, I was ready. It had been worth living just long enough to see her again. Suddenly, someone else appeared behind her and took her arm.

It was her boyfriend or something like that. I found it hard to imagine that anyone would dare to take possession of such a beautiful woman.

I know what you are thinking and I can see you smiling.

Do you think that I gave up?

I was unwilling to let this opportunity be wasted. Now I was determined. If I had ruined my first attempt because of my inexperience and my indecisiveness, I had been given a second chance and I was not going to waste it.

I was willing to rip a hole in the roof if necessary.

"Lord," I prayed, "if you are going to allow me to be a youth pastor to all of the young people of my country, first let me show you that I can be faithful with little. Before saving thousands of young people, let me rescue this poor woman from the clutches of that evil man."

After the service ended I quickly made a path through the crowd. The boyfriend moved away for a moment to talk to some of his cronies, leaving the door wide open for me. I know that this does not sound very spiritual, but I was deeply in love and I would be lying if I told you that I had decided to wait for a more opportune moment. I had made a decision. The young man who had entered the building on her arm was simply another obstacle.

He was a Jebusite trespassing on the Promised Land.

A Philistine defying the armies of Israel.

A prophet of Baal building an altar to defy the great prophet Elijah.

Another Judas Iscariot holding the bag with thirty pieces of silver and who would soon be on his way to a well-deserved hanging.

Now do I sound spiritual? I knew it.

I approached Liliana and went straight to the point.

"Liliana, I am Dante. I would like to introduce myself."

"Oh, yes, I just saw you singing," she said.

"No, no, no. We met a long time ago, about.... Five years ago."

"I don't remember," she replied.

To tell you the truth, I had prayed that she would not remember.

"I am sorry that you don't remember," I said, smiling. "We had an interesting conversation. But the important thing is that today is my last day at this church and there is something I have wanted to tell you for five years."

Liliana was watching me intently. All of the people around us seemed to disappear. This would be my only second chance, the one match that life seemed to be offering. If I were to ruin this moment, perhaps in another five years, or even less time, this girl will belong to another man.

There was a pause of five seconds, or maybe ten. But it seemed like an eternity. I felt like someone should go to the parking lot for a handsaw to quickly open this roof. The point of no return, either open the roof and send down the paralytic or else be kicked off the roof by the fisherman or whatever the name of her sometimes-boyfriend was.

"Okay, well, what I wanted to say was, and don't take this as a formal declaration, and I deeply respect that you are engaged. But what I am going to say is prophetic."

The Goliath was slowly approaching to interrupt our private conversation so I needed to hurry.

"Just to let you know, so that you are informed, I feel an obligation to tell you that I am the man of your life. In fact, you are standing before the father of your children."

What happened next was more than confusing. The expression on the beautiful woman's face changed from respect to surprise and then to anger in a matter of seconds.

The bells were muted and the doves flew agitatedly out of the sanctuary.

Liliana drew close to my ear, close enough that her Philistine would not overhear, and said: "I would never, never, never have anything to do with you. You are not my type. You are out of place and I am not attracted to you."

She turned around and fell into her boyfriend's arms.

But that was just a minor detail. I was determined. And while Thomas Edison had discovered two thousand ways not to make a light bulb, I was only on my first try.

So I ripped a hole in the roof.

I sent roses for her birthday.

I wrote love letters.

I offered her a job to help pay for her studies at the Bible school.

I made friends with her friends.

I sent messages.

I would happen to "casually" meet her as she was leaving her house.

I sent her more messages.

I took her hand with the sole and wholesome purpose of helping her cross a very dangerous street in Buenos Aires.

I called her on the telephone.

Later she told me that the Philistine belonged to her old life.

I sent more letters.

I endeared myself to her mother and impressed her father as a hard worker.

I stole a kiss.

Finally, she fell in love with me.

Six months and a few days after she had told me I was not her type, Liliana became my wife in that same church.

That beautiful woman gets more beautiful as the years go by and she has become the mother of our two beautiful children: Brian and Kevin. The doves still fly in our home and the crystal bells still ring. The perfect companion, the ideal woman, the woman of my dreams, sleeps with me.

Determination is the key. Whether you are learning how to preach or starting a business. To get that job or to earn that pay raise. To grow your ministry or to tell your loved ones the truth. To be an invader and not a passive observer. To go over things rather than allow circumstances to derail you.

You must arrive at your life's appointment.

Especially if you know that the Master is still in the house.

Even if you have to rip a hole in the roof.

CHAPTER 7

THAT STRANGE RACE OF VISIONARIES

The man walks among the tombs hunched over and silent. An autumn breeze is blowing in the cold cemetery. He is closer to the end of his life than to the beginning. He is living his last years, the best years, a time filled with experience. He looks tired yet he struggles to walk. Behind him some people who look like they might be family members watch him with deep respect. The man bends over one of the tombs.

The tombstone bears the name of a lieutenant in the American army. This was not just any lieutenant. To the old man, this name belongs to the one who saved his life. This lieutenant crisscrossed the globe during a time of war to restore his liberty.

Many years earlier, the American government upon reviewing the archives had discovered that one mother had lost four sons on the battlefront. It was decided that it would not be fair for this mother to lose her fifth son in the same way, underneath an army banner.

There had to be some way to compensate this mother and the best way to do that would be to find the fifth son on the battlefield, wherever he might be, give him an honorable discharge and send him home. Let him live out the rest of his years providing comfort to a mother who lost almost everything. During the rescue, the lieutenant himself could not believe that a whole platoon might be sacrificed to rescue one soldier. The attempt cost the lieutenant his life and the lives of some of his best men, and before he died the lieutenant looked the soldier straight in the eyes and spoke these last words: "I hope that you deserve this sacrifice, that you will at least live a life of dignity that is worthy of this sacrifice."

Now the soldier is the old man who is reading the inscription on the tombstone. The war ended many years ago, but he still wants to know whether he has repaid the debt he owes to the lieutenant. He looks at the tombstone and then he turns to his elderly wife, who is standing a few steps behind him, to ask a question.

"I need you to tell me if I have been a good man," he says. "Tell me whether I lived a good life. Tell me whether I was worthy of such a great sacrifice," he insists, and as tears run down his face the man and his wife seem to merge in an embrace.

This was the most well staged scene in the film "Rescuing Private Ryan," which featured well-known actor Tom Hanks in the leading role.

I have always been fascinated by the idea of trying to define the heart of a visionary. And possibly this scene from the Spielberg movie is what describes it best. Every dreamer feels like he is eternally indebted to the cross. He is aware that all is by grace, but even so, he still feels the pressure to make every minute count, every day of his existence.

Ryan could not allow himself the luxury of spending his life playing basketball or fishing in the river. A whole platoon of mean died so that he could live. He needed to do something important, something that would honor their sacrifice. He never invented anything. He did not win a Pulitzer Prize or the Nobel Peace Prize. But it was enough to know that at least he had managed to be a good father and a great husband.

This is a book for champions, for those who thirst after a gold medal, those who will not settle for less than first place. Basically, this chapter is for those who suffer from a holy dissatisfaction, for those who possess a double dose of spiritual ambition. Over the years, I continue to be amazed at how the meaning of the word "visionary" has been diluted. Anyone who builds a large church or launches a new project will not necessarily be nominated for honors in the hall of fame of those who were able to see beyond the crowd.

The visionary breathes, sleeps, bathes, dreams, laughs, and cries through the lens of his vision. He has no desire to start something only because a Sunday sermon touched his heart.

He walks in the supernatural realm even when the world is falling apart all around him.

I want you to see it this way: God does not celebrate birthdays or anniversaries and He is not governed by the clock. The Creator had already resolved the sin problem even before Adam sinned. Time is a framework created for mankind but not for God. He is in your present, in your past, and in your future. This concept may seem too childish and overly logical, but if you are able to grasp the concept, you will discover that God is the only one who can give you a word for the present that will heal your past and affect your future.

Of course, if, among other things, He has already been in your future, then he has already seen what is there for you in the years ahead.

Those who only see the present think that they discover their destiny. Visionaries have already gone on an exploratory journey with God and have already been there.

BACK TO THE FUTURE

Moses sends twelve delegates – one from each tribe – to spy out the land. Ten of them were crowd-pleasers and two were visionaries. Ten saw the giants, the other two saw the giants…and also what was behind them. Ten thought that God was asking for their opinion, two understood that they were given only a courtesy invitation, a chance for premium tickets to enjoy the show in style. When a good full-length motion picture is about to be released, the largest movie theater companies often arrange a premiere screening for a few well-known journalists, movie industry colleagues, performers, and other celebrity guests. They are not asking their guests whether they can release the movie. To tell the truth, they are not the least bit interested in hearing the opinions of the guests. They are inviting guests who they believe deserve to see ahead of time what millions of viewers around the world will later see on the big screen. That is exactly what Joshua and Caleb understood.

What God was trying to do was to offer them a glimpse of the future, a VIP (very important persons) pass to the first screening of what was to come. The Creator had organized a special event for his guests. But those who failed to understand were thinking that the film director had invited them to write a critical review of the movie for publication in an entertainment industry journal.

"We cannot do this, there are too many giants. It is too risky," the critics said, their eyeballs peering over spectacle rims.

"We can. We will devour them like bread," the visionaries said, enthralled by their journey into the future.

"We are like locusts in their eyes," concluded the spiritually blind critics.

"God will fight for us," reasoned the visionaries.

Now, I want you to read this carefully. You are may be about thirty-plus years old and still single. You may have begun to seriously believe that you will never marry. You cannot find the ideal man and you sense that you will die a "single old lady." The very thought of not having anyone with whom to share your love frightens you. I forgot to tell you that, in addition to being a preacher and a newly published author, I am also a mad scientist. I have invented a time machine and I want to test it on someone. If you would like, we could take a journey into the future, to perhaps the year 2020. I am not talking about a real machine. This is only a hypothetical journey to get an imaginary glimpse of your future.

Are you fascinated by the idea? I knew that I could count on you! You get into the machine and we push all the right buttons, calibrate the proper coordinates, and off we go.

Imagine that you can see yourself not only happily married but also surrounded by three beautiful children. To tell the truth, you have gained some weight, but that is not the most important thing. Watch carefully and, aha! There he is. He looks just as you had imagined, tall and good-looking. He is outside working in the garden. That annoying dog barks nonstop at the lawnmower he is pushing. Did you see that? You even have a dog, so you can really feel like a fortunate young woman. But we must return to the present. I never said we were going to stay there in the future. It is not your time yet. If you tried to stay there, you could interfere with your own fulfillment and find yourself alone with yourself, and that might cause a cosmic disruption. This is only a tiny preview of your life, a panoramic glimpse of what is to come.

Now, how are you feeling?

After having seen your future... Do you still believe that you should worry about dying alone, a single old maid? Of course not. You have been there and now you know what will happen. Now you can focus on enjoying the present and your singleness instead of regarding it as a curse. Let us agree that you have been transformed into a visionary. Now you have seen too much to let life pass you by.

Let's continue our experiment. Next in line, please!

Look who we have here. You look at me with a surprised expression on your face and tell me that you will never be a man of God. If I am not mistaken, you believe that you do not qualify for the spiritual championship. You have too many hidden habits to believe that God would have plans for your life. But of course, no one has told you about my time machine.

Come aboard and we will travel together to 2015. It is not that far away. Notice the imposing stadium in your future. Thousands of people are straining to get into the facility. They are coming from all over the world. Let's get in line with everyone else. No one will recognize us here. They are saying that this preacher is so powerfully used by God that several heads of state have asked for interviews. Even CNN is standing in line to get the best photographs of the crusade. And now, my distinguished time machine passenger, prepare yourself for the impact of what you are about to see. Watch as the preacher walks onto center stage.

Did you notice who he is?

I knew that you would not be able to resist.

You almost faint from the shock. It is yourself only a few years from now. The mustache does not look quite right, but the important thing is what God is doing with you. Paralytics who have been healed are running wildly around the stadium. People are gathering to pray the prayer of repentance for sins. The message you delivered was overwhelming.

But we must return.

Please, do not make things more difficult. I know that you would give anything to stay for the rest of the meeting, and see the fulfillment of your dream, but this was only a taste of your future.

I will ask you the same question that I asked the woman, now that we have returned. After everything that you have seen, how can you still worry about what your ministry will be or whether God is going to use you? The answer is obvious. Of course not. You saw too much to be satisfied with the small things of the present.

The visionary has already been where others have not dared to go. He has already seen the movie. All he has to do now is wait for the world premiere so that everyone else can enjoy the show. That is why those who are one step ahead, those who have already caught a glimpse of the future, can almost never enjoy the present.

Liliana, my wife, has taught me to live one day at a time. She often says that it is difficult to live with someone who has already seen the future, because he might make the grievous mistake of losing out on the present.

When God gives you a glimpse of your future and makes you almost drunk with a vision, it is so that you will learn to enjoy what you already have and so that you will be motivated to make every minute count, so that you will do something worthy of the amazing grace that has been poured out in your life.

The visionaries have an advantage because they have already been there, but the danger is that they will make the mistake of not appreciating their waiting room experience. Singleness only happens once. Small children will only be running around your house for a few short years. We must learn to live each moment knowing that we can never relive the past.

An old and well-known song popularized by a Latin American singer says:

I spent so much time running through life without brakes
That I forgot life is lived in the moment
Because I always wanted to arrive in first place,
I forgot to live and enjoy the little things.

The act of envisioning the future allows you to relax and gives you the peace of knowing that God is already involved in what is to come, and nothing and no one can change that. Joshua and Caleb counted on that truth. Even another forty years in the desert could not make them forget what they had seen.

SEEDS AND POST-DATED CHECKS

Imagine buying some tomato seeds. You remove the noxious weeds, fertilize the soil, rake the ground and plant your seeds. Every once in a while you dig up the rows, water your garden plot, and you wait. You are the only person who knows what is under the ground. You planted tomato seeds and that is what you are expecting will grow. When the time comes and your tomato plants emerge from the soil in search of sunlight, people who previously saw nothing will stop to compliment the fruit of your labors:

"Wow! What great tomatoes!"

"Who could have imagined that these beautiful red tomatoes would be growing in your garden?"

"My mouth waters just thinking about the great salad that tomato would make!"

Everyone is surprised. The whole world loves a good tomato. Neighbors come over just to see the plants' progress, the budding tourist attraction. They watch and delight in those incredible, inimitable tomatoes that have stirred the planet.

There is only one person who does not seem to enjoy them, or at least does not seem surprised: the visionary.

Don't blame yourself. It just means that you already knew what would happen. If you drove to the store and spent your own money on tomato seeds, you fertilized the soil, and you did everything that you thought you were supposed to do... What did you expect would grow there? The right answer is the logical one: Tomatoes!

While the neighbors are delighted to see your brand-new plants and imagine the healthy salads you will enjoy, you already have other projects underground. Other seeds are germinating and sprouting in the same garden soil.

That's what it's all about. The visionary has already been to the future and knows what will happen when the sun makes its next appearance on the horizon. He is not surprised to see a place where he has already been. This is why those who get ahead of themselves are often not able to enjoy their own achievements. They thirst for gold. They always want something more. They want to win the championship. They have no time to look at diplomas hanging on the wall. They want to go the extra mile. Another round. One more victory.

Before holding our first big crusade, I had a vision. The year was 1991. I remember that in the Spirit I walked all over that imposing Velez Sarsfield stadium. I traced every square inch of that place. I walked up every stair and carefully noted every detail of the facility. I imagined it filled with young people from all over the country. There was not even the remotest possibility that such a thing could happen. It was just an imaginary utopia. An unknown young man such as myself could never rent that stadium. Much less, according to common sense, should I dare to dream that I could fill that place with young people.

After the vision ended, I felt that I had effectively been there. I behaved as if it were logical that everything I had envisioned would happen. It was that simple.

I had traveled into the future and now I had returned to face the reality. When we finally held the first crusade in 1996, the only person who was not surprised was myself. The crowd applauded my tomato plantings, but I had already enjoyed this much earlier, when I bought the seeds of my vision. One of the secrets was that I believed in the seeds that I had purchased and, in consequence, I began to behave like the owner of a plantation.

I even remember what I felt inside after I had that vision. Nothing around me had changed. My life continued as before. The telephone did not begin to ring and no one came to our door offering a ministry position or a church job. But something inside me had changed. I felt like a "Youth Pastor." I only had a few seeds and only I was aware of what God was stirring underground, but the vision was enough to heal my self-esteem and to bring joy into my life. I changed the way I got out of bed in the morning. I began to sit up straight. My personality seemed to change and I walked with greater confidence. At that time, the largest crowd of people that had ever heard my preaching was a handful of young people, about fifteen, who boldly and bravely tolerated my inexperience. But I already felt like a preacher to the multitudes. I had been to my future and there was no doubt in my mind that it would happen.

Those are times when you bathe, sleep, breathe, love, and cry through your vision. A project is not the thing that keeps you going. It is your vision of the future that consumes every moment of the present. Can you identify with this concept? Let me tell you a little bit more.

We have already been through seven chapters together and I believe that I have gained your confidence. If I give you a check for a million dollars, a postdated check… can you have the confidence that you are a millionaire?

If you tell me no, you will deeply hurt my sensibilities.

If to you I seem like a trustworthy person, I do not see how you could doubt that you are a millionaire. The only catch is that you cannot have the money now. The check cannot be cashed for another year and two months to be precise. The check bears the logo of the bank, my authentic signature, and the six zeros that are necessary to round out the full amount. Now you must choose how you will live: whether cursing and wasting your present, or with raised spirits, standing up straight, knowing that in your pocket there is a check to cash.

When the date on the calendar finally coincides with the date written on your check, you will go to the bank and you will complete the transaction. If you have always had complete trust in me, obviously you will not be surprised. A very trustworthy person has given you this check and we naturally assume that this check is much more than a piece of colored paper.

If your vision comes from God, you do not have the luxury of doubting Him. He is trustworthy. His bank is solid. They even gave you a tour of the vault so that you could get a glimpse of the money inside that will be yours in the near future. The check is postdated.

Does singleness make you nervous?

It's just a matter of time.

Does it seem like ministries and gifts elude you?

Look at your check.

You cannot find an ideal job?

Call the bank and ask if your money is still there.

That prophecy, has it been delayed?

Take a small step toward the bank vault.

Are you not able to find the love of your life?

Fertilize the soil again.

Do you want to be part of a great revival?

Look at the picture of those tomatoes in your empty seed bag.

It is just a matter of time.

Visionaries often cannot enjoy the present because they have already been to the future. They are not satisfied with just one victory or one fulfilled dream, because they have already been there. And like that elderly man, Ryan, the former soldier, they feel like every moment of their lives is worth gold. They have an eternal debt to the cross and to the One who has taken them to see the years stretching ahead.

Do not look for a visionary at an amusement park. You will not find visionaries at large love fests or tedious fraternity meetings. Much less will you find them planning committee meetings for executive pastors. These people do not spend their lives playing tennis or watching television.

They are looking for a conquest. They want the gold medal, the belt, and the crown.

They are fifteen or maybe twenty years ahead of themselves. They belong to that strange race of visionaries and they have already seen too much to remain quiet.

CHAPTER

8

MEN IN BLACK

The two men are dressed entirely in black and wearing sunglasses.

They are walking at a brisk pace, and anyone can see that they are very preoccupied. In a matter of seconds a long hallway, dark and shadowy, almost sinister, seems to unfold before them as they proceed, a sort of premonition of what awaits. They almost never speak, but the two seem to be feeling the same emotion. It is an overwhelming and unbearable fear. Finally, one of the two men breaks the silence.

"Who will tell the boss?"

The other man does not answer. Only a murmur is heard. Perhaps he is clearing his throat. Maybe he senses that the inevitable is imminent. They cross a freezing cold passageway and a gate swings open with a spine-chilling squeak. There is almost no oxygen in the smoky room and the air is foul-smelling. The dark visitors can only see the imposing red throne from behind. They can barely make out the silhouette of their supervisor standing in a thick haze. One of the men in black is sweating profusely. The other man is so gripped with fear that he finds it hard to breathe. The boss does not ask any questions. He only waits in silence for their report.

"We could not do it," says the man who cleared his throat. "Better said, there is nothing that we can do."

The boss continues with his back to them. He has not said anything, but they know that he is very angry. He tends to lose control of his temper when he hears that a mission has failed. That is why the men in black are trembling. But this time there are no shouts, no hysteria. The boss still has his back to them and they perceive a deep sense of frustration in his words. He sounds tired. Barely, almost imperceptibly, he moves his large, bony fingers.

"They must have some weak point," he says, "an Achilles heel. Are you sure that you tried everything?"

"Everything, boss. We have filled them with temptations around the clock. We have tried to fill them with feelings of guilt and self-pity, but without results. We have tried to fill them with hatred and resentments, but those disgraceful people have found an antidote. We have exhausted all of our weapons trying to fight against them.

"They must have some curse or weakness!" says the shadowy, dark figure of the boss, raising his right fist. "Remember, they are only mortals. Have you tried impure thoughts and obscene photographs? The weapons of pornography and obscenity are always effective in destroying them!"

"That doesn't work on these people. They get up every time. They have the stamp of a new generation. They are fearless, part of the latter rain squadron. They are a latent threat to us. We cannot seem to break them. They always live in a state of alert. Their hearts are the hearts of brave knights."

"I know," the boss replies through clenched teeth. "As long as young people continue to rise up, we will not have a moment of peace. The worst part is that they are no longer content merely with self-defense. Now those disgraceful people are attacking us."

"Also, they are continually receiving training, boss. They are preparing for war. They are being trained to fight without mercy, without truce, and if this continues, they will raise up others like Him. They will ravage the schools, the universities, the workplace. They will not be just playing at evangelism, these Christians will be passionately involved. Completely radical. They have lost their fear of us. And they seem to have learned where the real battlefront is."

"If only they had stayed within their four walls singing choruses. They would be defenseless. We have seen entire generations lost in just that way. I can still hear those poor little sheep begging for mercy."

"Are you joking? This generation is not content merely with social gatherings and silly fraternity meetings. These people thirst for conquest and will stop at nothing. They thirst for the gold. They want to be champions. They are simply different. They want to invade everything in the name of Je... well, in the name of you know who."

UNDERNEATH THE BOXING RING

Not long ago, I was told the story of a well-known pastor, a friend of mine. He was invited to meet with a committee of pastors and theologians. They had been intrigued by the sermons of this distinguished orator and went straight to the point. They told him, no holds barred, to give them a good reason why he never mentioned Satan in his messages. He never referred to the devil or to his host of demons.

The preacher leaned over in his chair and made a gesture as if trying to remember. After a very long pause, he frowned and said:

"Satan... Satan... that sounds familiar. If I remember rightly you must be referring to the one who, according to the Bible, was conquered and cast down by the cross. Am I correct?

The others silently nodded.

"Then you will have to forgive me," he added. "I spend so much time with God that I do not have any time left to spend on those who have been defeated. My vocabulary does not allow me to include the losers."

Those who were present at that meeting say that no one was able to discuss or add anything to what the man of God had said. His reasoning was impeccable.

Over the years, and at times for entire generations, we have spent far too much time in fear of the devil. Even after we come to know Jesus Christ, we subconsciously fear that at any moment the opposing team may still win the battle. Entire bestselling books have been written in which the author page after page tries to define and discuss the enemy.

The common denominator that I have encountered every time that God has placed me in front of a multitude of young people is that terrifying, implicit fear that they often feel toward Satan. Spiritual warfare seems to be the one and only secret weapon that is absolutely vital and necessary for living a victorious live and experiencing true revival.

It is as if the Lord had said that he was able to defeat the enemy a little bit, but because he was not able to finish the work, we must complete the conquest.

I want you to carefully read what I am trying to say:

Satan is defeated.

Powerless.

Defeated.

Through.

Finished.

Destroyed.

On the ropes.

The cross put an end to that bully.

And one big secret: Satan is afraid of champions.

When a champion boxer has earned his title, he never has to fight again if he so desires. He no longer has anything to prove. He has managed to defeat those who were competing for the belt. But if someone should challenge him for the title, the only person who can authorize a new title match … is the champion himself. If the owner of the crown does not authorize the match, it does not matter what the challenger says. He will not be able to enter the ring.

As soon as you understand that through the grace of God and His redeeming sacrifice the Lord Jesus has given you a champion's belt, absolutely no one will be able to enter your ring. You will be at the top. Holding your title. The only thing the loser can do is to try and challenge you from outside the ring. But he is not at your level, unless you give him permission.

In the Garden of Eden, God sentenced the serpent to crawl in the dust. That is the level where the enemy belongs: slithering on the ground. He is not even in the ring with you, and the only one who can let him in is you, yourself. When you can understand the full meaning of these words, you will discover that the enemy is not worried about attacking you; he is too busy defending himself.

The odd thing about spiritual warfare is that we stray from the mark when we attack. On that fateful day, September 11, some evil people had as their goal the destruction of one of the most important architectural landmarks in the Big Apple, the Twin Towers. Their twisted minds never contemplated trying to murder the architect or the designer of the towers. No, their target was the building itself, standing as a symbol of the nation's financial strength.

Many Christians believe that spiritual warfare can be reduced to scolding demons or shouting orders at the devil to leave the premises, but in reality they are only targeting the architect or the designer of an evil system and doing nothing to hinder the enemy's work. As long as we waste our valuable time on useless, hysterical screams, the diabolical system will continue dragging souls into hell.

The problem is no longer Hitler; it is Nazism.

The problem is not the devil; it is his system.

When our goal or objective is not clear we sometimes mistakenly think that we are battling Satan, and that is when we start to get scared. But that is exactly what he wants. That is the method that he uses to get you to leave the ring or to give him permission to get inside. We forget that what is in us is greater than anything outside. We believe that our victory is only temporary because, sooner or later, the enemy will come back for revenge. We think that we can never be champions, ignoring the champion's belt that by God's grace girdles our waists.

I am not saying that you should not be alert and aware, but remember that the Creator has made a place for you. You should no longer waste any time listening to all the dummies shouting and screaming outside the ring.

STAR WARS TOYS

Let me explain it this way. I am the father of two wonderful boys: Brian and Kevin. Therefore, I can rightly consider myself an expert in video games (I don't play them but I know all about the genealogical tree of Mario Bross). I could take you on a guided tour of my son's bedrooms and tell you all about the Spiderman and the X-man. These last fictional characters are not easy to understand, but I do know that Spiderman is hopelessly in love with his neighbor.

Obviously, I also know everything there is to know about animated figures feature films. I am almost considered an expert in the genre. I have seen those full-length movies hundreds of times, I know all the songs, I know the secrets of the Lion King, and I know why the Beauty loves the Beast.

But there is one movie in particular that reminds me of some Christians I know. It is called Toy Story. More precisely, the one and only Buzz Lightyear is my favorite character.

Do you have any children? Then you must know what I am talking about.

You don't have any children? Then you should have some. You cannot go through this life without experiencing this fascinating film about the world of toys.

The script tells us about the lives of a child's toys and the love that they feel at knowing they are part of his childhood. They are only toys and they know it except for one: Buzz Lightyear, a robot who has only recently arrived at this house. Buzz believes that he really belongs to the Star Command and is convinced that his arrival in this child's bedroom was caused by an error in his spaceship's navigational coordinates. The poor action figure believes that he really is fighting in a space war and that he must defend himself using his "paralyzing laser beam."

"Do you really think that is a laser beam?" asks an incredulous little cowboy the size of a Barbie doll. "Don't you know that is only a miniature flashlight? You are a toy!"

But Buzz prefers to believe that he is guarding a powerful secret weapon in his right hand. He also believes that his box is his spaceship. He is absolutely convinced that he comes from a galaxy far away, even though on his back are the printed words "Made in Japan." Finally, another toy gets sick of Buzz and takes off his space helmet. Buzz believes that he will die if he breathes the oxygen of planet earth. He starts choking and he goes into convulsions and spasms, until finally he realizes that it is all an illusion. The air is not hurting him. To tell the truth, he will soon discover that he is not a superhero from outer space … just a new toy in a long series of toys.

Through the years I have seen many Christians who look like Buzz. They could live normally, but they prefer to believe that they come from a galaxy far, far away. They need to recognize that their packing box is the unending grace that allows them to walk and make decisions, but they prefer to think that it is powerful. They forget that they have the telltale words "Made by God" stamped on their backs, preferring instead to believe that they are star fighters in an intergalactic conflict. They could be salt and light in a place of bland mediocrity and darkness, but instead they never take off their transparent space helmets in order to avoid worldly contamination.

And of course, they spend their time aiming their tiny little flashlight at the enemy thinking that they are wielding an enormous, paralyzing laser gun. They yell and rebuke, they make geographical maps and they symbolically conquer cities. They are living out a war that has never been declared when they could be recognizing their own status as champions and raising their arms in victory inside the ring.

The devil may be walking around like a roaring lion circling the winners, but he cannot touch you if you have your belt in place. And besides, a lion that roars is often the one without claws or teeth and is just making noise. He has no authority to pick a fight with you if you do not permit it. You are his nightmare and not the other way around.

When we finally understand this concept, we no longer waste our time beating on an architect who is already defeated. Instead, we target the perverted system. But the Buzz Lightyears, instead of making a difference in society, prefer to attack the enemy with their tiny colored flashlights.

Why should they try to change the course of a government that has become corrupt by invading the political system, much like Joseph did in Egypt, when they can berate the nation's rulers from the privacy of their houses?

Why should they try to change a nation's unjust and discriminatory laws, attending the university to prepare for a career, when they can spend their lives playing a keyboard and singing in a church?

Does it make sense to prepare yourself to serve as an incorruptible judge, an impartial attorney, or a businessman who invests in the kingdom of God, when you can merely do a symbolic walk seven times around the proverbial Jericho and then spend the rest of your time watching television at home?

Laziness disguised as spiritual warfare. You fail to commit to a world that is in the throes of agony, and yet you pretend to be involved in intergalactic warfare. You are waving little colored flashlights, pretending they are laser guns, when you should be developing a counterculture.

We do not win the war by attacking the designer of the system. We do not win the title by challenging someone who is already defeated. We cannot give ourselves the luxury of continuing to fight against Satan when the real problem is his works.

A well-known speaker once said that we often take out of context the idea that no one is saved by works so that we will not have to love others, so that we will not have to get too committed.

True champions are not trying to gain a victory, they are simply holding onto their titles. The belt is something that the true "Hero" has given you purely by grace. It indisputably enables you to take first place.

Now, as the champion, you can use your influence to change some things. You can revolutionize the faculty or change the system at your workplace. You can change your city's codes and prepare for the big leagues of government service. You can turn the tables on the entertainment industry's penchant for selling sex by generating new ideas that are revolutionary and holy. You can demonstrate that it is possible to be rich without being an embezzler or an unscrupulous operator.

Oh sure, you can also choose to seal out contamination by wearing your space helmet and playing intergalactic war games.

A journalist friend of mine who is a highly respected professional once said that some Christians remind him of a certain father of a family who goes to buy a new car.

It is the car of his dreams — powerful, a German brand. He parks the new car inside his garage and takes off the four tires, replacing them with wooden supports. He then invites his wife and three children to get in the car for a ride. He starts the engine, cranks up the car stereo, turns on the lights, and steps on the accelerator. In a matter of minutes the garage is filled with smoke from the exhaust and the horrible smells of burning oil and fuel. The roar of the engine mixed with the music inside the vehicle creates a deafening cocktail.

The dream car is making a lot of noise but it is not leaving the garage: it lacks wheels. The eccentric owner of the brand-new car is not unlike some Christians who do not understand where the real spiritual battle is being fought. The noise and the music alone will not intimidate the enemy. The smoke and the smell of burning fuel will not frighten him.

Now, accompany me once more to that dismal place described at the beginning of this chapter and listen to the rest of the conversation.

The men in black are silently watching their sinister commander and respectfully waiting for an answer.

For the first time, the boss stands up. The mist is still overwhelming and dense. A deep sense of foreboding fills that place. The boss looks at his two best emissaries and orders them, with a shake of his finger, to get out of his sight. He never wants to see or hear from them again. He knows he has lost and it hurts his demonized pride.

"I cannot allow them to destroy what I built with so much effort," he says. "Losing to a bunch of theologians is more dignifying and even entertaining, but I cannot fight against a whole generation spread through an entire city."

No one says a word in the fields of hell. There is nothing to celebrate or to add when their mission has failed. Satan contemplates his defeat, powerless, and his servants tremble with fear, much fear, perhaps because they know that a new generation is being trained to be victorious or to die in the attempt. And also, perhaps, because they suspect that they are not going to get any respect.

The champions are inside the ring.

And the men in black tremble with fear.

CHAPTER

9

THE DIVINE SHOWMAN

The children are afraid of him and the women of the city never talk about him. The heads of households advise their children to stay away from him. They say that he is very dangerous and that no one knows what he is capable of doing. They call him the "Crazy man of the cemetery," although a few people say that he is really not schizophrenic, only tormented by an old demon. This is all part of an urban legend circulating around the small city. Although he is a nuisance to society, an indigent, he is still part of the rusty and aged demographics of that morally ambiguous culture.

On some eerie nights at camp meetings, seated around a bonfire, the most incredible stories are told of that sinister person. One old patriarch told his grandchildren that many years ago, a group of inexperienced young men had gone to the cemetery and tried to bind the man with chains. But the crazy man broke the chains as if they were silken threads. They say his superhuman strength is diabolical.

It is said that at one time he was a well-known attorney, but that he went crazy after he found his wife cheating on him with his best friend. Others deny that story and say that he is the product of a mother's pact with Satan, that she gave him up for wealth and riches, that she left him abandoned next to a tombstone when he was still a child. Others swear that he saw his son commit suicide and could never forgive himself for not spending more time with him, and that is why he cuts himself with stones until he bleeds. A more powerful story is the one that says he was once a wealthy magnate from a distant country and that his ambitious wife induced him to take strange drugs that took away his mental faculties and pushed him to a life of vagrancy. He wandered the world until he found a resting place in the cemetery of that city. Whatever the truth may be regarding the "crazy man of the cemetery" who lurks amid crumbling tombstones, just a mention of him chills the hearers' blood. But in only a few minutes someone will change this urban legend forever.

The Master emerges from the boat with a little smile on his face. Someone behind Him is telling a joke, perhaps Peter, who is trying to entertain his friends after a night of hard work. John is tethering the boat while Thaddeus is still thinking about the storm that had almost destroyed them during the night as he moves their baggage to the shore.

Suddenly, the morning calm is rudely interrupted. A man looking haggard and out of sorts is shouting wildly. He is naked, grimy and caked with dried blood, and his body emits a foul smell. Peter tries to protect his Master, while some children, well acquainted with the sight of the crazy man, giggle from their hiding place behind some rocks.

But the Master does not need a bodyguard. Unexplainably, the unusual attacker falls to his knees in front of the Master and begins to plead. He begs for pity. Some curious neighbors cannot hear what the man is saying but they can see him from where they stand. The crazy man. The stranger. The subject of urban legend is talking to someone who seems to know who he is, even if He does not live in that city.

The man who has so recently arrived is asking some short questions and then signals toward a herd of swine. His gestures are not pompous; they are precise and direct. Suddenly, about two thousand swine seem to go crazy. The animals are squealing loudly, biting each other, and then, amazingly, they stampede toward a rocky promontory and throw themselves into the sea, committing suicide.

The "crazy man of the cemetery" now stands to his feet. The curious onlookers see him smiling for the first time. Someone hands him a coat and suggests that he bathe himself at the seashore. Miraculously, the man is in his right mind. And the Master continues to smile, watching as the last of the drowning swine disappears under the water.

He could have liberated the Gadarene man in some other way, perhaps in a more formal manner. Perhaps the Master should have laid His hands on the crazy man and caused him to fall to the ground unconscious until he was free. Or perhaps he should have taken the man to the local temple and prayed for him in the prescribed way, without a lot of fuss. But that is not the Master's style. Jesus Christ is innately creative. He is an innovative and unstructured showman.

Do you want to continue watching this drama? Come with me to the other side of the city and you will split your sides laughing at what you see next. A blind man approaches Jesus to ask for healing. Once again, the surprise factor. He could have simply placed His hands on the blind man and healed him. Or He could have ordered Philip to play the keyboard and "set the stage for miracles to happen." Perhaps He could have breathed gently on the eyes of the man who could not see. But that was not His style. Jesus looks askance at the doctors of the law who are watching him from a distance, standing near a tree nearby. He is also aware that other inquisitive Pharisees are watching from behind the dusty glass panes of a window. He wants to hold their attention. And then he has an idea. An innovative and brand-new way to heal. He spits on the ground and makes some mud with the saliva, improvising a mud patch for the eyes of his newfound acquaintance. Then the blind man is sent to the Pool of Siloam to wash his eyes. A few minutes later, the blind man is shouting to the four winds that his sight has been restored. The curtain comes down and the stunned crowds of people are giving a standing ovation as this somewhat eccentric Son of God returns the greeting with a smile.

The disciples cannot get used to His style. They cobble together a huge luncheon feast with the fish and bread that Jesus has multiplied as if by magical arts. He is invited to a wedding and the best He can do there is to change water into great wine, the fruit of an excellent harvest. He tells His friends to go ahead of Him in the boat and then meets them halfway through their journey, walking on the water. He is creative, an innovator, a consummate stage artist.

It is incredible how, throughout history, we often forget the details of God's divine creativity. Perhaps this is because as ordinary human beings we don't like change. We like what we know, what is traditional, the standard. For that reason, God tells Jehoshaphat to put down his weapons and assemble an orchestra while his enemies are busy killing each other. Perhaps for that same reason He tells Joshua to take some unusual walks around Jericho. Or He tells Moses to keep his hands raised high in order to make the difference in the battle. Undoubtedly, God did not use up all of His resources during the six days of creation; He continues to generate innovative ideas throughout history. That is why the Son shows the same creative qualities when He appears on the scene. And that is why we should see some creativity in ourselves as well. But unfortunately, many people think that creativity is a form of disrespect.

The champions in any discipline, those who have made their mark on the history of humanity through the centuries, are those who imprinted a new style on everything they did.

And, obviously, they generated controversy.

"But why do your disciples disregard the traditions of the elders?" The unbelievers asked this question because they could not imagine anything ever changing. They loved tradition and venerated the sacred doctrines, they were devoted to following the law, but still they lost sight of the Son of God.

Religious tradition was the intellectual author of the crime of Christ's death. The Romans were merely the executioners. This obedience was required by the theologians of the time.

A CHURCH THAT MOVES BACKWARDS

It is incredible to see thousands of young people locked in a prison cell of routine. Without creativity, without taking risks, jammed full of methods that have already been tried, wrapped up in tradition or in "just because."

The young Christians of today look back at past generations and believe they will revolutionize old dogmas by moving standards from one side to another. They believe that they can let the divine creativity flow by dancing until they are drenched in sweat or by acting out some choreographed moves to the beat of the newest praise chorus. Others consider themselves pioneers because they are members of a Christian rock band or they preach without wearing a tie. But the music is not the thing that will make you an innovator. Even wearing that Hawaiian shirt when you stand on the platform is not going to make the difference. Creativity is not a position or a posturing. Creativity is the flow of God's power in our lives, even if it is not always shared by the conclave of tradition. About ten or fifteen years ago the thought of hosting an evening concert or a dance choreographed with scarves or banners might have been considered heresy. But now such events are regarded "moderately acceptable" forms of worship within certain contexts.

We have our own language, our own songs, our own way of greeting each other and even our own style of clothing to some extent. Everything fits perfectly. We know what is permitted and what we should not even think about.

One idea for a creative, innovative worship meeting might be to feature a message presented by a troupe of mime artists. After the artists perform a three-minute pantomime, accompanied by a song, the youth pastor might feel obligated to apologize in case anyone was offended, explaining that this is another form of preaching and also explaining what the mimes were trying to say in case no one understood their gestures.

In my opinion, an evangelistic meeting of Christians ought to be composed of three long hours of praise, one half-hour of worship, a short announcement explaining the need to take up an offering, and finally the sermon, not forgetting, obviously, to conclude the service with another half an hour of what seems like never-ending praise music before finally dismissing the congregants. The most innovative churches might even consider organizing a concert. Stage the event with lots of colored spotlights, smoke machines that produce a suffocating haze, and a sound system capable of perforating the average eardrum. We often imagine that is the greatest, most creative way to try to reach the world for Christ. But someone has to give us the bad news: "The church is still living in the 1970s." We are doing everything we should have done thirty years ago. Our dogmatic clock is lagging horribly behind the times and, sadly, few have noticed there is a problem.

The mindset of the average Christian tells us that if something works, we need to repeat it over and over again for the next twenty years, until everyone is sick of the same old thing. I cannot imagine the disciples just going through life looking for the "crazy men of the cemeteries" or herds of demonized swine. I also doubt that anyone ever thought of organizing a "spitting" on the ground program to benefit blind people in the region. Or a new denomination based on the concept of turning water into wine.

We are enamored of what has already been done. Someone has already paid the price of innovation before we heard the story. We often prefer to imitate rather than to create.

Not long ago, I took a famous movie producer to a Christian service. He considers himself a follower of the Lord "from a distance." But he had never visited a church. His life's work is devoted to designing and building scenery for large theater shows on Broadway and in some of the largest capital cities of the world. We can safely assume that his expectations for any show are very high. We met during our most recent evangelistic project and became friends to some extent. At least he accepted my cordial invitation to attend a Sunday church service. The service began a half hour after the announced starting time. Someone was testing the microphones over and over again while the musicians warmed up and frantically tuned their instruments. The drummer seemed to be working out his anxieties after a bad week by beating on his instrument even before the first song had begun. Finally, a young man invited us to stand and sing praises to God. The first song lasted about twelve or fourteen minutes because we repeated it over and over again — first by women only, then men only, then all together, then a capella (no instruments), with clapping, then without clapping, and finally everyone together again.

My friend had a serious look on his face. The young man who was leading the service had asked us to hug two or three people near us and to greet them with words like: "Prepare for the anointing that will come upon you tonight and will fill you with joy" or something like that.

My friend became even more serious. There was another song. None of the musicians were smiling. Instead, they all seemed to be in a trance or, in a worst-case scenario, thinking about something else.

Someone else went to the pulpit and again asked us to say something to the person next to us and to two or three people around us. Then he asked for a clap offering. The keyboardist had not understood the signals so the pastor asked for another round of applause, something that would allow time to tell the keyboardist what to do.

My friend whispered in my ear that he was leaving.

While he was trying to make his way out of the church building, I was amazed to see the young speaker was again telling us to say something to the person next to us and asked us to jump around and make some war cries.

In our culture, this might well be considered a great praise service well worth remembering. But for the man who had just entered a church for the first time it seemed like a huge crowd of improvised yelling, lacking in creativity and common sense. My guest is a well-educated man and tried to excuse himself, but I was interested in hearing his point of view. I realize that I could have focused entirely on the religious issues. I could have told him that he "does not understand the things of the Spirit" and I also could have convinced myself that he had resisted "the anointing and the glory." But I preferred to put myself in his place and try to hear him out. Perhaps I could learn something.

"I was surprised," he said, "that nothing was prepared or rehearsed mainly because this is for God, as they suggest. For one thing, when I hire musicians, they have an obligation, by contract, to smile when they are acting. These people… were only playing music. Besides," he added, "they seemed disconnected, without any idea of what to do next."

I was left speechless and trying to think of an explanation. But I realized that reform was needed. We need a radical, drastic change in our dogmas and customs.

If a movie runs longer than two hours, we feel like our brain is going to explode. The same thing happens if a show lasts longer than one and a half hours. But we are known to hold religious services lasting five or six hours.

One time I was asked to preach in a country that I love, at an event that was to take place at the main stadium. The meeting began at 10 o'clock in the morning and it was five o'clock in the afternoon. Already three speakers had preached to the crowd without any break and I was the fourth speaker on the schedule.

"Relax," was the emcee's advice of sorts. "Here the people are used to this." But the crowd was not that "accustomed." The people were unbearably hungry and mentally exhausted. As one preacher friend of mine often says: "The heart resists when the tail bone suffers."

I warmly greeted the people and then sent them to rest after I learned they had already been there for seven long hours.

We have no creativity. We are lacking in common sense. We plan church services and conventions to suit ourselves, but we scare away the unconverted. We hold events aimed at those we imagine will understand our intentions, but we forget about the one who truly knows us and who understands what we were trying to do or say.

URGENT REFORM

Just for a moment, observe Jesus again. In less than fifteen minutes he has healed a leper and preached a sermon. He astonishes the crowd and holds their attention in the palm of His hand. He monopolizes the attention of the learned and the well educated. Both the elderly and children understand Him and will push and shove to get close enough for a smile or a wink from the Son of God.

He goes to another city and again creates something new. He changes His style, revolutionizes local customs, generates controversy, and shreds tradition to pieces. He can draw from an arsenal of divine knowledge and astonish the theologians, but instead he prefers the simplicity of parables.

He makes the people laugh, comparing faith to a mustard seed. Or he tells the rich man that a camel has better possibilities than he. He is full of surprises. He is not saying something: He has something to say. But even though He does not seem controlled by a program, that does not mean He is improvising. Give a blank sheet of paper to a religious man and he will complain that he has nothing to read. Give the same blank sheet to an artist or writer and he will be grateful for providing materials with which he can work.

Unfortunately, many Christians let someone else fill their blank pages with someone else's handwriting. They do not let themselves dream of something new, because they believe creativity reeks of heresy. I have spoken to dozens of young people who can only imagine two ways of serving God: preaching or playing music. If they have no musical talent or do not have the confidence required for public speaking, they feel excluded from the team, shut out of the big leagues.

Our dogmas and belief systems need a drastic overhaul similar to that generated by Martin Luther. I am not talking about a posturing of gratuitous transgression that wounds the senses, but rather a reformation based on biblical principles and one that is calibrated with the desire of the Lord's heart, that of winning lost souls.

We discover praise music and we become worshipers of worship. We make a cult out of the newest song as if this were a magic formula for bringing down the presence of God. We are legalistic about freedom: if you do not jump or dance, you are considered weird, a spiritually cold fish who is out of sync with the move of God; when in reality those who are out of sync are those who cannot decipher the religious codes of the insider.

We are still living in the 1970s, still repeating the mantra that God never changes and that we should not imitate the world. To say that God never changes is to be ignorant of God's style of creating new things, and to emphasize that we should not imitate the world is counterintuitive. Every moderately intelligent Christian knows that Satan is the imitator, not we ourselves. And in any case, his clock is ticking right along with the times while we are the ones running terribly late.

We refuse to change our church services, but we are too impatient to watch an antiquated black-and-white movie. We enjoy Hollywood's special effects together with our children, but we still think that unconverted young people will come running to our church services just because this week we are introducing two new worship choruses.

We are amazed at the elaborate scenery of any theatrical production done by Disney, but our concept of appealing to unbelievers consists mainly of dancing crazily to the rhythm of worship songs. We are left open mouthed by the eloquence of a politician, but the sermons we preach are extracted from a book of sermons written a hundred years ago. We complain about the high price of movie tickets and then the movie starts ten minutes late, but we are able to schedule a church service for seven o'clock and then we delay opening the service until the people start to arrive.

We would easily jeer at Lucian Pavarotti if he were to sing out of tune during one of his operatic performances, but we applaud the worship leader who sings "off-key" to the glory of God.

We demand a refund if the comedian forgets his lines or tries to hide his mental potholes with the request: "Greet the person sitting next to you and say: 'How nice to have the chance to see such a funny comedian,'" but we willingly do this hour after hour if it is all for the Lord.

I am not against the greetings and the praise and the shouts of joy. It is just that our church culture is not impacting those who do not know God. We understand it, but the unbeliever outside the church can barely tolerate us.

Two years ago I met a youth pastor who was not achieving the success he hoped for with his youth group. In spite of his good intentions, he did not seem to have much influence over his people. We worked with him trying to discover the problem. Suddenly, I thought to ask him a question. "What is your dream? What are your future aspirations?" The young man stared at me in shock, stunned that I had asked such an obvious, self-evident question. "I want to pastor a congregation. I want to have a church and I want to conquer my city." That was his problem. Instead of focusing on innovative ways to reach the hearts of his young people, he was using this position as rehearsal for his true vocation. For him the youth department represented the minor leagues. This was a place where he could practice for real ministry. And that attitude was blocking his success.

The young man dressed like his pastor. He grew a beard to look older than he was and ran his youth group meetings much like Sunday morning services.

When he spoke on the radio, instead of talking to an audience of young people, his remarks were directed to the ears of the pastor, so that he would be "regarded as a great preacher in the making." Instead of focusing his energy on the young people, his efforts were aimed at getting promoted to another position in the main church. God cannot add a special anointing to your work when you are mentally packing your suitcases in preparation for a different calling. Tradition and the desire to imitate what he has seen working for others are propelling him toward imminent failure. He is taking a shortcut to hollow tradition. He will achieve his pastoral goals, found his own church, and then believe that he has seen the fulfillment of his dreams, when in reality someone else is filling his blank pages and has told him, subconsciously, what he is supposed to do.

We live out of sync with our times. Thanks to the Internet our young people have instant access to all the information they need. The remote control for the television has become just another extremity, an extension of our nervous systems, and if something is boring we instantly push the button. The new millennium has overwhelmed the senses of our young children. And if the church is unaware of these changes, we will continue to use archaic methods and waste our evangelism efforts.

THE GOD OF ORIGINALITY

In June of 1991, my wife and I felt the Lord leading us into a youth ministry. Our first idea was to start a radio program focused on youth. But we knew we would not reach the hearts of young people using a traditional format. They probably would not listen to another preacher for an entire hour, interrupted every fifteen minutes by a long list of meeting announcements. We began to pray fervently and then we let our creativity soar. We spoke of the sufferings of a man of God through a series of programs titled "The Thoughts of the Pastor's Dog." We meddled with the spiritual health of a fictional character, half carnal and half Christian, who was called "Cristianeitor." "The Adventures of the Super Deacon" made us reflect on the ups and downs of participating in church meetings. Dozens of such episodes made our program entertaining and educational at the same time. Within less than six months ours was the most popular program for young listeners. In fact, "The Show for Young People" is now broadcast on five hundred radio stations in twenty-two Spanish-speaking countries, becoming one of the largest syndicated radio broadcasts in Latin America.

In the summer of 2002 we introduced a multimedia evangelistic show at one of the most well known theaters in Argentina. Our team presented a one-and-a-half hour program that included stunt doubles, 3-D special effects, fiber optic streaming, set changes, elaborate costuming, laser lights, and topnotch actors. We called it "Mission Rec" (Mission Control Recovery) and it received rave reviews from the critics in local newspapers and magazines. Obviously, a certain percentage of those people who cling to tradition saw it as a complete heresy, but we were encouraged to see that hundreds of people leaving the theater had become fertile ground for receiving the gospel message.

We had to work hard, rehearse constantly, and synchronize the work of the actors with the timing of the special effects. But it was worth the effort. While I am writing this chapter, we are negotiating with a large company to finance a "Misión Rec" tour of every province in Argentina and other Latin American countries as well.

A famous show producer told me that our program would be a failure because we did not have any naked women or off-color language. After the premiere, after seeing the long lines of people waiting to see the show, he must have realized that divine creativity is far superior to his corrupt and obscene scale of values. This new reformation does not necessarily have anything to do with producing an innovative program for radio or television. Rather, it requires a drastic change in our way of thinking. We need new wineskins that will not burst so that the new wine of the Spirit can find its habitation inside us.

There are hundreds of ways to serve God and to maximize your potential. You can become an actor and win a little statue for "best foreign picture," showing that you can make a movie that appeals to the entire family. You can win the World Cup as the best soccer player in history without the use of anabolic steroids or stimulants. You can produce content and promote new ideas to a television audience that feels devalued and without resources. You can be an excellent politician or steward of your country's commodities instead of praying that corrupt presidents will repent or handing them Bibles that will only be stashed in some closet. You can be a business professional or a bank manager who is able to finance large evangelistic projects.

But in order to do all of that, you must prepare.

A champion knows that training is vital and determines the outcome. When you are overwhelmed with the desire to serve God "full-time" and to "live by faith," resist the temptation to take a shortcut and study. Prepare yourself. Work hard. Go for the gold. Do not aim for anything less than first place.

In order to experience a true reformation, we will need qualified radio announcers, excellent conductors and journalists who are full of intellectual ability and anointing so that we no longer have to get by with those mediocre Christian programs produced by dear brothers who have good intentions but little else to their credit.

We need to find different ways of preaching the gospel message for a variety of television audiences; if not, our Christian television options will be limited to preachers who make it easy to flip on the television set on Sunday mornings instead of making the effort to attend church. In our day and age, we have amazing communications technologies that are of concern only to the preacher and his family, a couple of grandmothers and that one person who watches Christian television all day long so that "God may bless this house." We do nothing to produce. We generate no ideas. We have nothing original to say.

Now, put your hand over your heart and answer me truthfully. You don't have to answer intelligently. Just tell me what you are really thinking.

Do you really think that your unsaved friend and businessman would sit through one of our never-ending Saturday night services? Do you think he would miss his favorite program to watch our Christian television channel? Do you really believe that he would understand one word that spiritual leader on the radio is saying?

If the thought "No way" immediately crossed your mind, then you may agree that we urgently need a new reformation, a change of direction in our concept of how to win the world for Christ. Finally, I want you to stop and read the following dialogue. This story is true and verifiable.

"I think that you need peace in your life and the only way to have peace is to have Christ…"

"I don't believe that. I feel very peaceful. My life is full of relaxation."

"Well, perhaps you are having financial problems."

"No, I don't have that problem. I am a millionaire."

"Ah … But when you are feeling alone…"

"I never feel lonely. I have a wonderful family to keep me company."

"If you get sick…"

"Never. My medical team is able to prevent any health problems."

"Well then, I will come back to preach to you when you need something."

Do you think this is fiction? Then you are wrong.

Not long ago while visiting the Dominican Republic I met a Christian who had had that very conversation with a well-known secular singer. Before that his only method for sharing the gospel was to appeal to some need the unconverted person might have. But when he met someone who thought he had everything, he did not know how to talk to him about Christ.

Success is not about a salesman persuading the barefoot man to buy a pair of shoes. No, success is more like talking the connoisseur of shoes into buying yet another pair.

The debtors, the desperately poor, the disheartened, the woman who has just learned that her husband is unfaithful, the young man who tried to commit suicide last night, all of these people will willingly endure our five hour long church meetings. They will do whatever we tell them. They will nod their heads at things they barely understand and they applaud whenever we ask them to. But there is another group of people outside the church. These are people who do not understand us even when they try. They are entrepreneurs, university professors, intellectuals, and very busy people. These are men who depend on the fluctuating value of the stock market, people whose cell phones never stop ringing, businessmen who risk their lives with postdated checks, a critics always looking for a good show.

These are people who think they have it all – a wife, two children, a house, two cars, a dog, and a weekend lover. These people need Jesus Christ just as much as that drug addict who visited the church last night. It's just that no one knows how to tell them. We have the best product, but we are lousy salespeople.

Maybe we need to take another look at the Lord.

The Master is walking down one of the main city streets and a large crowd is gathering behind Him. A cold drizzle is mercilessly falling on the people. Suddenly, one of the disciples realizes that they must stop at the corner to let a funeral procession go by. Four neighbors are carrying the coffin. And a woman is weeping uncontrollably as she caresses the cold and lugubrious box. She does not even suspect that the Creator, the one who placed the stars in the sky and contained the sea at its shore, is watching her.

Jesus stops at the corner and interrupts the procession. Simon Peter grabs his head and looks askance at the family members who are angry at this meddling.

But the Master is hiding an ace up his sleeve. Once again He will break down barriers. He tells the woman to that there is no reason to cry. An onlooker is angry at His lack of respect but then the muffled laughter of an adolescent boy can be heard.

Yes, the Lord is creative. He is an innovator.

He touches the coffin and tells the occupant to rise. Now the one who was dead is smiling and asking where they are taking him. The woman, who is the mother, faints from the emotion.

The neighbors cry out in terror and those who were contracted to perform the funeral service are angry about losing an income opportunity. Many of the people who are following the Master experience a mixture of wonder and fear.

But the Lord cannot be defined by a single method. He simply works wonders. He is not predictable. He is majestically strange and improbable. The disciples have been following Him for three years now and they still cannot figure Him out. Until now, no sermon has been identical to another, no service like any other. He displays the style of great geniuses. He is like the Father.

An Eternal and Divine Showman.

CHAPTER 10

THE AMAZING STORY OF THE COHENS

"If you had to describe what you do, all in one word, what would it be?"

This question was thrown at me without prior warning by a producer at one of the most important television stations in Puerto Rico, and I must confess that it made me stop and think.

At one time the press in my country had baptized me as the nation's "Youth Pastor," but this nebulous "title" generated a certain amount of resentment among those who were saying that you must have a church to call yourself a pastor. My denomination had, a few years earlier, granted me the credentials of a preacher as a form of recognition, but to be honest, I don't feel like that title quite explains what I do. I also do not consider myself a writer (in fact, I still don't understand why these editors continue to believe in me).

Every time I am asked to list my occupation on immigration papers I feel like I am faced with a huge dilemma. Sometimes I call myself an "artist" (I have been a cartoonist ever since I can remember), but if the mood strikes me, I may call myself a "conference speaker" or else simply a "communicator."

I love to tell stories and to write them. One of the biggest pleasures of my life is to see people absorbed in the message, carefully following every detail as I preach.

I believe that one of the most difficult art forms is to capture everyone's attention and to touch their hearts with a fascinating story.

A dear pastor and friend of mine, one who knows my weakness for a good story, keeps me stocked with them. His name is Italo Frigoli. I consider him to be one of the best speakers of the last twenty years. He is an excellent husband, lover of Italian pastas, lives in Chile, and is the director of an up-and-coming soccer team. Italo sometimes calls me on the telephone and says to me, in his most oratorical voice: "Dante, I have a story and I know you will really be able to get the juice out of it with your style."

Then, without having to pay for the movie rights, he hands over another stick of dynamite, another story that really puts me into action. The one that I am going to tell you now is one of those. When my friend from the other side of the Andes mountains told me this story, I knew that I had to include it in this book, perhaps because every champion should know when the time is right for making a decision.

But before we dive into this fascinating story, I should clarify that over the years my wife and I have always maintained a certain "holy paranoia." Our biggest fear is that we could do something that God did not tell us to do – that we could move out of God's will and get ahead of His plans for us. Perhaps this fear is because we know the benefits of being in the center of His perfect will. Because of this, we are terrified at even the thought that we might stray from His design for us.

History can testify that many great athletes at the peak of their careers have signed the wrong contract. Presidents have placed their seal on bad decrees. Actors have taken roles in a bad script and an even worse film project that pushed their careers into oblivion. Boxers have continued to fight when they should have retired on schedule. Preachers have made big mistakes on a project that was not birthed by the heart of God.

If someone wants to experience victory, they cannot take anything for granted when making even the most basic decisions. That is why I want you to come with me on this journey to get acquainted with a certain person. I have always believed that this could have happened.

He is robust, wears a thick reddish beard and is about forty or so years old. He has a Latin air about him, although there is not much possibility that he was born in America. His name is Philip Cohen and he is the husband of Rebecca (a sweet and good-looking woman) and father of five wonderful children between the ages of five and fifteen.

The Cohens are a typical family. He raises cattle, takes out the trash, has a Great Dane for a pet and in his free time plays golf. She is an excellent cook, loves her children very much, and has a weakness for seafood. To tell the truth, the Cohens never would have made history if they were not one of the many families making a sort of exodus journey through the desert. Our new friends are on their way to the Promised Land and an old patriarch named Moses is leading the way.

To be more specific, for fourteen years now they have been traveling in circles around this interminably vast and arid desert. A cloud guides them by day and a column of fire protects them at night. The work ethic is more than simple: As long as the cloud stays put, all of Israel remains camped underneath it. If the cloud starts to move, then everyone packs up and follows. In other words, they are nomads until further notice.

The Cohens have already grown accustomed to this lifestyle. In fact, their children do not know anything but the white sands of the desert. The only break in their weekly routine comes when the guards announce that the cloud is moving. Only then is reborn the hope that they are perhaps getting closer to their destination — the famous country that Moses has promised over and over again they would someday see. That is what the Cohens' life is all about. Camping, packing the suitcases, gathering the livestock, unpacking the suitcases, and then setting up camp again until the next signal.

But something mortally serious is going to occur in the lives of the Cohen family. Something that the story tells us marked them forever. A crack. A surprising and unexpected turn of events.

They say that it all started one day with a private conversation between husband and wife in the bedroom, at around eleven o'clock at night.

"I am sick and tired of going around in circles!"

The wife's words startled Philip who was trying to skim through the newspaper after an exhausting day. At first he thought this was just another one of his wife's usual mood swings, perhaps a sudden hormonal fluctuation.

"I said that I am sick and tired of going around in circles in this dry desert." She is serious. This is not simply a trivial statement about who should be watering the gladiolas. Rebecca is upset. And she has already said it twice.

Philip lowers his newspaper and tries to think of some encouraging response.

"You know that we are all going to the land that God promised us…I don't think it will be much longer."

What is your concept of 'much' longer? Fourteen more years? I want a different future for my children, a stable home. I need a permanent address so that regular folk will know where to find me, a place where I can post all my photographs so that my grandchildren can see their grandmother's house. I don't want to be a gypsy for the rest of my life!

I don't want you to be confused or to get a wrong impression of the woman. There is something logical about what she is saying. She is exhausted. She wants to stop traveling, to settle down, to belong somewhere.

"I understand," says Philip, caressing his wife's long hair. "But we are living under God's cloud, under His protection. We have been following His direction for fourteen years just like the rest of Israel. It is too risky to think about…"

"To think about our children? Is it too risky to think for once about us? Doesn't it seem a little strange to you that we never arrive at this famous 'never-never' land? How can you be sure that Moses is in his right mind? What if the sun has burned out his brain cells and we are at the mercy of a crazy idealist?"

Philip has been married for several years and he knows when his wife is serious. He also knows that he would rather confront an entire army than challenge the woman with whom he shares a bedroom. There is not much more to say. Rebecca wants to stop following the caravan. She wants to stay right here, without any further discussion.

"When the cloud moves again, you can follow it if you want. I will stay here with the children," Rebecca concludes before she rolls over and turns out the light.

Very early the next day, the guards announce that the cloud has begun to move. Thousands of campers are preparing for another exodus. Everyone is racing against the clock, all except the Cohen family. The night before the Cohens made an important decision: They will not follow the cloud.

The neighbors are overwhelmingly surprised and stop by to find out the reasons for this strange attitude. In all these years, no one has ever had the audacity to stay behind. Mister Cohen tried to give an explanation. He says that he is tired, that he will dedicate the rest of his life to his wife, that he does not share the vision of the majority. To tells his closest friends that he does not agree with the Moses' leadership, and reemphasizes that his decision is permanent.

About four million Israelites parade past the door of Philip's tent. Everyone is wondering why this family is not moving. The Cohen family is the talk of the day. The Cohens will be staying in the desert.

After the last ray of sunlight disappears behind a huge mountain of sand, the Cohen family can be seen silhouetted against the horizon. The Cohens have remained alone in the middle of a vast wilderness. The silence is absolute, almost deafening. Philip breathes deeply and fills his lungs with fresh air several times.

"All in all, it was not a bad decision," he says.

They no longer have to wait around for a cloud to tell them what they must do. They also are not dependent on Moses or his occasional bouts of lunacy. They no longer have to put up with annoying neighbors or the gossips across the street. It was not such a bad idea after all.

THE COLDNESS OF THE SOUL

It is now finally dark outside and they should already be in bed. Rebecca hardly says a word, she only smiles, grateful for the unconditional support of her husband in making this monumental decision.

"It is a little cold," the oldest child says.

It is true. The temperature continues to plummet. Rebecca makes her smaller children put on their coats and she gives the five-year-old, who cannot stop shivering, an extra blanket. The night air is getting so cold that it is frightening. They are chilled to the bone. The cold air blows right through the holes in the tent. Critics of the Bible often try to say that there never really was an exodus through the desert. They say that no human could withstand the extreme temperature swings, the boiling heat days and the freezing cold nights that are so typical of the desert. What the atheists do not understand, and neither did the Cohens suspect, is that the cloud of glory, which became a column of fire by night, maintained temperatures ideal for human habitation.

Now the cloud has gone away with the rest of the people of Israel, and besides, the family's tent has no heating system.

The Cohens lost the fire.

I have always said that no one stays cold for fun or because they wanted to be cold. The greatest failures are always preceded by small cracks. Just one little wrong decision may someday lead to our souls freezing over. We allow ourselves to make a mistake, a compromise, and later one evening we discover that our prayer life is stunted. We try to organize our thought life by ordering our minds not to be distracted, until finally we fall asleep. The fire of His divine presence is only a beloved reminder of our first steps. The Bible begins to seem dull and monotonous. The verses that previously encouraged us now seem like obscure and meaningless hieroglyphics.

Sermons don't taste the way they did before. They now sound predictable, redundant.

Praise songs now sound bland and insipid and we no longer see any reason to attend church.

Finally one Sunday we discover that it will take a superhuman effort just to put on a tie or a good dress to go to church. And that is the day when we begin to die a little. The cold begins to freeze our hearts.

The Cohen family has endured the worst night of their lives, certainly the coldest. Finally, the first rays of the sun appear on the horizon like a long-awaited gift. Rebecca leaves tent to look for the daily ration of manna. A healthy breakfast will do much to revive the family's downcast spirits following a horrible night. But the morning light holds a bitter surprise for them: There is no manna to be found.

"It's impossible," Philip reasons. "In fourteen years we have never gone without food!"

What he did not realize was that the manna came from the cloud. Now that they are not under the cloud, they also have no provision from God.

A bad decision will affect your wallet. A wrong move, a wrong answer on the spiritual chalkboard, could mean an empty table. Bills you cannot pay. Salaries that do not go far enough. The dark specter of unemployment. Battles that leave us feeling defeated and intimidated. Credit cards with interest rates that overwhelm us and checks that bounce for lack of funds.

It's just that, I am sorry to have to tell you, in God's will there are no magic formulas. If you are not in His perfect will, you are left without a contract and excluded from the big leagues.

But Philip Cohen has Latin blood. And someone like him is used to surviving on very little. "Maybe God wants us to fast," he may say. He believes that God is working on them. He says that he wishes God would tell him, but he isn't hearing anything. Incredibly, he is calling a disastrous situation that he himself created a "test from God." A crisis always sounds better when it is disguised as reverence because if we call it by its true name, it is a "product of disobedience."

Rebecca decides that they should at least drink some water, or tea perhaps. Human beings can live quite a long time without eating, but they will not survive long without water or at least liquids.

However, the first rays of sunlight have already evaporated any trace of water. There is no cloud of God's presence. There are no miracle rocks from which water might be gushing. There is no Moses here, no neighbors around who might have a little water stored away in a canteen.

This certainly is a bad day. Even so, Mr. Cohen has not lost hope. He believes that anyone can have a round of bad luck, but tomorrow everything will be different. Even though there is nothing for supper, the couple and their children hold hands around the dinner table for a short family devotional.

"God could not have forgotten that we served Him for many years," Rebecca reasons through her tears.

This is not about bad memories of God. It is about finding the right place. In God's university, you are not graded on a curve:

• "Well, let's see ... they are out of my perfect will. They have decided to do whatever they want, but I must remember that they have served Me well in the past."

• "This time they did not prepare for ministry, nor did they seek my face, but I will bless them for old times' sake."

• "He has decided to take me out of the way and find himself another wife without consulting me, but nevertheless I will bless his future marriage because in his previous relationship he really was seeking my direction."

Even so, Mr. Cohen tries to say a prayer as the head of the family. But it is Rebecca who notices that their youngest child is more flushed and red than usual. His skin looks a little sunburned. She goes to him, touches his forehead and discovers, to her horror that the child is burning with fever. To tell the truth, the middle child also seems to be suffering from sunstroke. Her daughter is complaining that her face and head hurt. The oldest son takes off his shirt to reveal that his back is completely covered with sores.

"This cannot be happening," says Rebecca, interrupting a prayer that had only barely begun with great difficulty. "In the last fourteen years the sun has never harmed our children!" Perhaps she has forgotten that the cloud also sheltered her children by filtering the sun's damaging rays.

THE INEVITABLE FAREWELL FROM THE HOME

When, on a certain occasion, they told King David that his son Absalom had died, the king raised his voice so that everyone in the palace could hear his words, words that might be considered an epitaph for his dead son. "My son, Absalom, I wish I could have died in your place!"

These were the saddest words ever expressed by the psalmist, perhaps because nothing compares with the pain of losing a child.

Without a doubt, God willing, we may not have to say good-bye to a child from the vantage point of parents standing around a coffin. But we all, without exception, will have to say farewell to a child who is leaving the home.

Have you not experienced this aspect of being a father? Then you have surely experienced this as a child.

On that fateful day a child leaves his toys behind to become a man. At first, this just means changing the posters on his bedroom walls. He says goodbye to Barney and Mickey to make room for football stars or a popular singer. Later, almost from one day to another, he will introduce you to his girlfriend. This is the woman with whom he will share the rest of his life. A perfect stranger will dare to take your son away.

"Are you sure you are ready for marriage," a mother might argue. "You know nothing about life; you are only thirty-eight years old." But that day, sooner or latter, will come knocking on your door.

On that day our daughter, in whom we have deposited all of our dreams, first tells us that she has a boyfriend, and that she is bringing him to our house to meet us. But I know what you are thinking.

That boy is not worthy of my princess. She deserves something better. Am I right? He doesn't have a good job, he seems immature, he has too many freckles and, besides, you don't like how he looks at your daughter.

"He has a lustful look in his eye," you tell me. And I must give you the benefit of the doubt. Your experience as a father has taught you to beware whenever someone looks at your daughter in that way and tries to undress her with his eyes. Perhaps this is because you recognize that when you were a bachelor you had that same look in your eyes. The day will come when you will see a reflection of yourself as a young man.

Perhaps you will not have to say goodbye to a child dressed in black suit or white wedding dress. Perhaps your child will leave home to live alone or will need to move to another city to study. Or perhaps a divorce means you will only see your child on weekends.

It is then, and only then, that we will remember those bad decisions that may have marked our children's lives forever, things that affected them in childhood.

We may feel regret for those words we spoke in moments of anger. There were times when we ignored them or when our schedules or our jobs took so much of our energies that we were too tired to stop and play with them.

"I wish I could go backward about fifteen years and fix my relationship with my son," we may be thinking.

On the day when we say goodbye we would give anything to turn back the clock, to stop the sun from moving across the sky, even if only for one week. Life has kept us so busy for so long that we have lost our children.

Now your son no longer wants to play football with you. He is twenty-two years old and he has other interests. You will not have another chance to attend his graduation, to congratulate him on his grade in mathematics, or to scold him for spilling ink all over his notebook. Now he barely talks to you. The separation is so extreme that it has been a couple of years since there has even been a conversation between father and son. You are almost strangers to each other. When he was a child, he was your buddy and you were his Superman. Now your son is a power player trying to negotiate for his own territory and you are his dictator.

At some point in time there was a "crack" in the relationship. Something broke on the road to adulthood. Our children as kids think they know everything. But do you really want to know the heart of a man? Ask his child.

They watch you in times of victory ... and also in times of defeat. They know how their father reacts when things are going fairly well and also when the pressure is on. They know that you are a hypocrite ... in the hypothetical sense, of course, just in case you are one.

They are silent witnesses who seem absorbed in watching television while their father is mercilessly criticizing the church. The child may not seem to understand very much when his mother gossips about the leaders and the vision of the church. But they hear everything, even what is said behind closed doors.

"I don't criticize," you say. "It is just a family matter."

But your son does not understand these semantic details. He stores absolutely everything in his little heart. And some day, when he leaves home, everything that unconsciously affected his childhood will put a tarnished frame on a grayish relationship between father and son.

It will not do us any good to be famous, to develop a ministry, some recognition, a good house, or a church full of people who love us if we have earned the scorn of our own children.

The bad decisions of these parents, Philip and Rebecca, mean that their children are suffering from severe skin damage.

The mother can see the blisters on the skin of her young one and blame the youth leader. Or perhaps the church that was not able to keep his attention. Or perhaps the youth department did not have a good program. Or an even easier excuse, perhaps a demon has taken possession of him. But in any case, Rebecca knows the truth: If you have abandoned the protection of the cloud, do not ask for protection for your children.

Perhaps she thought that if she were not following Moses, her decision would adversely affect only herself. "It is my decision, I am an adult and what I do does not affect anyone else," she may have thought.

But she forgot about the generational curse. She overlooked the wellbeing of her own family, of her young children, of those who would innocently pay the consequences of her wrong decision.

Finally, the Cohens look at each other and, without any need to say more, they know what to do next. They pack their suitcases as quickly as possible. The light of the moon illuminates the darkness, allowing them to gather their things. They have decided to rejoin the others, to again take shelter under the cloud.

Suddenly, in the distance, they hear the thunder of horses' hooves galloping on the sand.

—Perhaps someone has missed us,— Philip thought.

But these travelers are not their former neighbors. They are bandits, foragers. They often follow closely behind the encampment looking for any scraps that people may have left behind. They would probably steal everything that the Cohen family has left, rape the wife and children and perhaps worse.

According to the story, the Cohen family members dropped everything they were carrying and ran into the shadows of the night, heading toward the protection of the cloud.

No one knows for sure whether they got there in time. Some say that they traveled all night and by the next morning had rejoined the group on the other side of the mountain. But others say that it was too late. It was impossible to run in the desert with five children. For that reason, this is an open-ended story. In reality, we will never know what happened.

Nonetheless, if at night you feel the chill air of spiritual stuffiness, perhaps your hunger for something from God is becoming unbearable.

Your thirst for His presence has left your mouth dry.

Your finances are in poor shape.

And your family is unprotected and exposed to the horrors of life without God's protection.

Then, my dear Cohen, run for your life.

A champion could lose everything if he is not where he is supposed to be. If you start running now, perhaps it is still not too late for you.

EPILOGUE

THE
DISSIDENT

THE DISSIDENT

The defendant waits silently in the dock.

He does not seem anxious or worried. To the contrary, at times he almost seems to be hiding a smile, as if he knows something that no one else does. He is wearing blue fatigues and even though he is not wearing a full-dress military uniform, he gives the impression that he may have some military ranking. This case is unprecedented.

The judge is known for being fair and impartial and everyone trusts his sober judgment. The dry thud of the gavel announces that court is in session. The prosecuting attorney, in a stylish black suit, makes his case.

"Judge, honorable jury, we have before us a clear case of someone breaking the law. For reasons that have something to do with his religious convictions, he refuses to conform to the traditional lifestyle of this honorable community. Society is a sort of ecosystem where if everyone obeys the established rules, the wheels turn and function perfectly. But at times," the attorney adds, in a more hushed tone of voice, "people appear on the scene who want to alter the established order of things by raising the banner of revolution and working against the rules and what has been long accepted as the norm in our culture."

"We need you to clarify your allegations," the judge interrupts. "We don't have a lot of time."

"Of course, your Honor. To be perfectly clear, the defendant has tried to organize a 'new revolution' to counteract the system. He has recruited more people than any politician ever dreamed. He has invaded our schools, faculties, offices, and factories with a message that is completely antithetical to the things we have been taught since earliest childhood. He calls abortion a crime when it is nothing but a choice of lives. He labels as sinners and adulterers those who adhere to the free expression of legalized divorce. He defends virginity while ignoring that sexual pleasure is the right of every citizen. He continues to complain that the nation lacks integrity, raising doubts about the morality of those who govern our country.

"Objection, your Honor," says the defense attorney who, oddly, is wearing a white suit. "The prosecutor is not being specific or timely in his accusation. We are not here in this court session to pass judgment on value systems and ideals.

We must go directly to the crime in question.

"The defense attorney is right," says the judge, leaning back in his imposing chair. "Explain yourself more clearly, mister prosecutor."

"Of course. The accused says he is 'sick' of hypocrisy and peccadilloes. He claims to defend values that are downright prehistoric such as blind obedience to and respect for parents and fidelity between marriage partners. These values would co-opt the free expression of our young people. In addition, he wants to ban certain offensive expressions from the public media, a proposal that smells of repression and censure campaigns from the past that no one wants to relive. He also denounces corruption and immorality as if he were the only one with the moral authority to do so.

"That is ridiculous," the defense attorney says calmly. "You cannot accuse someone for simply pointing out a difference of beliefs about society. Democracy and true freedom are not synonymous with license. There is no legal basis for the charges against the accused."

"Welcome to the system, my dear attorney," the prosecutor responds, his voice dripping with irony. "People such as the accused are only making everyone else uncomfortable. The majority of people only pretend to live in harmony with the national order. But he is a countercultural revolutionary. He is opposing the established parameters. And what makes this case even worse is that he has already convinced many people to support his ridiculous standards."

"What the prosecutor is trying to say," the judge says, hazarding a guess, "is that the accused, instead of yielding to the pressures of society, has chosen to live his life by a different standard, even placing his own reputation at risk. And," he adds, as if already knowing the answer, "he is saying that he does not care about popularity and having a good name as long as he can support a cause that he considers just, even if this cause goes against the grain of current cultural trends and the general consensus."

"Exactly," the defense attorney responds as he walks slowly past the jury box. "This man stands accused simply because he has brought thousands of people back to true integrity and to values that were already established long before this perverse system changed the value system for every human being.

"It is time to decide whether these values are right or not," the judge replies tersely.

"The point is not that he may have jeopardized his reputation," protests the prosecutor as he nervously adjusts his tie. "What makes this matter of grave concern is that this man has recruited dissidents all over the country and his movement has grown to include numerous groups that are organizing to train a new squadron of rebels."

"For goodness' sakes, prosecutor," the judge interrupts. "We are not here to talk about evangelism methods. This discussion has become irrelevant. I find no cause to condemn a man just because he is different. I don't believe that this will destroy our system. The state cannot condemn someone only because he is different or, even less so, because the people who embrace his cause have done so entirely of their own free will. Society has seen thousands of idealistic young people like this man pursuing visions of utopia or following illusions that eventually died.

The judge motions almost imperceptibly and then someone

is calling the accused man to the witness stand. He will have only a few minutes to say something in his own defense. His words will need to be concise, incisive, direct. The young man begins to speak.

"Judge, members of the jury, ladies and gentlemen.

"Today you will decide whether you will let me preach and officially promote my truth. Another option is to mark me as a dissident of the system that you control. But you should know that you will not be able to break my will. I will always be there, in the new reformation of the church. When no one believed in me, someone decided that I could play in the big leagues and gave me an opportunity I do not want to waste. I have worked very hard to change my destiny and to promote a cultural revolution for this generation. Every morning of my life I struggled against a hidden addiction until I conquered it. Every minute of my life, I have breathed the vision of changing thousands of lives with a radical message."

Suddenly the courtroom is filled with a deafening uproar. Some opportunistic journalists are trying to immortalize the accused man's face with their photography, flooding the courtroom with the glaring flashes of their cameras. The judge pounds his hammer, requesting silence.

"I understand that my methods are a little unorthodox," the young man continues, "but I have decided to oppose what the manual of spiritual health, the Bible, declares to be perverse and noxious."

"Don't be confused. You do not have just another face in the crowd standing here in front of you. I was trained for special missions. I am determined to conquer everything in the name of the Lord who has placed this trust in me. I can start over and over again, even if you put a price on my head."

"Decide for yourself. You either have a colleague who will fight for a new generation, or a thorn in your side. Unfortunately, I cannot go against my code of ethics. I would rather die trying than to retreat from my commitment..

The judge now looks like he is not breathing. You can almost cut the tension in the room with a knife. Only a few nervous looks from the audience are noticeable as people look around the room trying to see whether the words of the man accused of revolutionizing the system are having an effect. Then the judge leans toward the microphone and hands down his sentence.

"Time will be the best judge. If this revolution is just another movement like so many others it will dissolve of its own accord just as other false movements that have disappeared from the scene without further ado. And if there really is something different, something better in this movement ... no one will be able to stop it. We could condemn this young man and a thousand would rise up. We could throw a few people in jail, but this revolution is already spreading throughout the nation like a flood. Instead, we will let history be the judge of these people. As for me, I have no other objections. I declare this defendant unimpeachable.

Court is dismissed.

The gavel hits the bench amid a deafening murmur. The judge, confused, retires to his chambers. The defense attorney, dressed in an impeccably tailored white suit, winks knowingly at the defendant.

The dark and controversial prosecutor curses and pounds his fist on the table. Journalists, reporters, and photographers are trying to get some final remarks from the defendant amid a flurry of flashing cameras and pushing and shoving.

The defendant continues smiling. He has not opened his mouth throughout this uproar, but he is smiling. The honor code of champions does not allow him to make statements to the press. He stands to his feet, amid congratulations from bystanders, and walks toward the exit. This young man is only in his twenties, but his maturity is astounding. Outside these doors the revolution and the cause await his return. The banner that will change the system. The squadron of resistance. Those who do not want to be influenced by a sick society. Those who will be accused time and time again and will continue to smile quietly, knowing that the man in the snowy white suit will always be there to defend them.

As the defendant was leaving the courtroom, a photographer snapped the portrait of the dissident that appeared on the front page of the local newspaper. Now I am asking you to look very carefully at this photograph. Focus on the young man who is pushing his way out of the courtroom amid a jostling crowd of journalists.

Only those who notice the finer details will see the fire in his eyes. It is a sacred flame, impossible to imitate. It is the look of conquerors, of visionaries who are born to win. These are the eyes of a knight armed for battle. He is part of a new generation. But if you look again, you may notice one more detail, almost imperceptible.

Get closer.

Watch carefully.

Look beyond his eyes.

Dig deep into the heart of a lion.

He is unbreakable.

This is *The Champion's Code.*

ABOUT THE AUTHOR

Dante Gebel is well-known as a bestselling author as well as conference speaker and preacher who currently serves as pastor of the Hispanic services at the Crystal Cathedral in California. Gebel has reached millions of television viewers through his programs that are broadcast on several television networks. He has held several massive events, called "Super Classics for Youth," at various stadiums throughout America. Dante is recognized in the Hispanic world as an outstanding speaker ministering to the youth and the family, a leader well able to entertain with fascinating stories that leave the audience laughing to tears. Dante currently lives in Orange, California, with his wife Liliana and their four sons: Brian, Kevin, Jason, and Megan. Visit his official website at: www.catedraldecristal.org.

The entire Gebel family (from left to right)
Right of Dante: Brian (drummer and artist); Liliana (queen of
the family); Kevin (who dreams of receiving the legacy of his
father, to be a preacher); Megan (the princess); and Jason (the
young computer amateur).
Currently, the family lives in Orange, California.

ABOUT 90,000 YOUNG
AND THE SAME PASSION
BY JESUS

An image that summarizes the miracle of seeing thousands of young people filing a stadium to hear the message of "The pastor of the youth".
(River Plate Stadium, Buenos Aires, Argentina / 2005).

THOUSANDS OF HANDS
RAISED TAKING
A COMMITMENT
HOLINESS

"If you really want to, you can change your star".
Thousands of uplifted hands of youth who believe that they
can cease to be invisible, and become invincible, if they adopt
"the Champion's Code".

OTHER BOOKS
BY THE AUTHOR
(IN SPANISH)

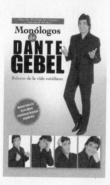

NVI Bible With
Author's notes

By The Author's
Wife

We want to hear from you.
Please send your comments about this book to:

Vida@zondervan.com
www.editorialvida.com

THANK YOU.